# micro-PROLOG and Artificial Intelligence

**More Books on Computer Languages and Artificial Intelligence**

*LISP*
*The Language of Artificial Intelligence*
A.A. Berk
0 00 383130 2

*Classification Algorithms*
Mike James
0 00 383054 3

*Pattern Recognition*
Mike James and Vartkes Goetcherian
0 00 383187 7

*Introducing C*
Boris Allan
0 00 383105 1

*Exploring FORTH*
Owen Bishop
0 246 12188 2

*Introducing Pascal*
Boris Allan
0 246 12322 2

*Introducing LOGO*
Boris Allan
0 246 12323 0

*QL SuperBASIC*
A.A. Berk
0 246 12596 9

# micro-PROLOG and Artificial Intelligence

**A.A. Berk**

COLLINS
8 Grafton Street, London W1

Collins Professional and Technical Books
William Collins Sons & Co. Ltd
8 Grafton Street, London W1X 3LA



First published in Great Britain by
Collins Professional and Technical Books 1985

Distributed in the United States of America
by Sheridan House, Inc.



*British Library Cataloguing in Publication Data*
Berk, A.A.
micro-PROLOG and artificial intelligence.
1. Artificial intelligence—Data processing
2. Microcomputers—Programming 3. Micro-Prolog
(Computer program language)
I. Title
001.53'5'0285424 Q336

ISBN 0–00–383158–2

Typeset by V & M Graphics Ltd, Aylesbury, Bucks
Printed and bound in Great Britain by
Mackays of Chatham, Kent

# Contents

# Preface

This book is aimed at introducing the important artificial intelligence language of PROLOG, which will also form the background language of the fifth generation machines. The particular dialect of PROLOG around which the book is based is called micro-PROLOG, and is by Logic Programming Associates. Many thanks are due to LPA for their encouragement during the research for this book, and to both LPA and Acornsoft for allowing me to see and use their pre-release version of micro-PROLOG.

The facilities described here are those of micro-PROLOG for any of its implementations, which range over most of the popular machines and operating systems on the market. It is largely due to this LPA version of PROLOG that the language has begun to gain such an extensive application.

The examples in this book are based primarily on natural language, and the manipulation of lists of words. Later chapters introduce the type of programming needed to analyse and 'understand' natural language, an application for which PROLOG is better suited than the majority of other languages in existence.

To understand this book fully, you should already have some familiarity with a language such as BASIC, but no great depth of knowledge is needed, as the two languages are rather dissimilar. However, you should have an idea of the basic concepts of computer programming, and appreciate how important it is to think logically.

Finally, I should like to thank a number of people for their assistance during the work on this book – first, my patient wife and family who have to put up with my distracted temperament while working, and who bear the effects with great understanding and even encouragement. Secondly, I should like to extend my sincerest thanks to the staff of Collins, and Sue Moore and Richard Miles in particular, for their continued patience, encouragement, and outstanding professionalism.

A. A. Berk.

# Chapter One
# Initial Principles and AI

## Introduction

Many books and languages claim to be orientated towards artificial intelligence (AI), but what does this mean exactly? The present book aims to answer this, and many other questions, while at the same time giving the reader a grounding in one of the most important AI languages.

The main problem is that intelligence, whether artificial or natural, is not yet defined. Even workers in the field have difficulty in explaining the meaning of intelligence, and its rigorous definition still thoroughly eludes us.

One of the aims of AI, which should always be borne in mind, is to understand ourselves and our mental powers further, and perhaps to help in improving them. AI continually seeks analogies between human behaviour and computer programs. Furthermore, because we all possess this indefinable attribute called intelligence, we are all well qualified to form an opinion on its structure.

Though AI is still embryonic as a subject, there is no shortage of languages in existence for experimenting with it. PROLOG is one of the most successful to date, and this book provides an introduction to an important microcomputer dialect of the language – micro-PROLOG. Its importance as a computer language is underlined by the statement that the new fifth generation machines will rely heavily on the use of PROLOG.

To provide the reader with a sound basic feeling for the meaning of an AI-orientated language, we will see here the attributes which a successful AI language should have. This will also introduce some of the main attributes of micro-PROLOG for further detailed description in the succeeding chapters.

## Artificial intelligence

There are many areas within AI, but some areas are more popular than others. For instance, there is much talk at present about *expert systems*. This is effectively a method of capturing – within a machine – the expertise of a specialist, and using that knowledge to aid less specialised people to gain access to that knowledge. The facts and expertise which are to be used by the computer are held in a special type of database, generally called a 'knowledge base'.

The prime attribute which separates an expert system from a simple database is the system's ability to use its knowledge 'intelligently' or creatively in some sense. As an example, it is easy to produce a manual on the working of a complex piece of machinery. If the machine is faulty, and must be taken apart, a human can refer to the facts stored in the manual. This gives his intelligence the necessary body of facts to find his way through the complex process of pattern matching the data in the manual with the machinery he is working on. The use of the facts in the manual still requires a high degree of expertise on the part of the user.

An intelligent manual, however, would actually interact with the human, suggest lines he should take, accept input from the human as to the progress so far, and perhaps accept a statement of the symptoms of the problem to be corrected. The system would then be in a position to link some of its knowledge data together and suggest a line of attack. These are things which even the most uneducated human is able to do with ease. Humans are able to form opinions based on previous knowledge, test those opinions, update their present state of knowledge, and then try out new opinions as a result. These attributes are some of the ones which an intelligent expert system should possess.

It is well known, of course, that a bunch of facts does not constitute intelligence. It is the way in which those facts are put together, or used, which gives a system or a person intelligence. Intelligence, therefore, is much more bound up with the ability to provide links between facts, and perhaps build up new facts from old ones, than simply repeating data verbatim. We say that 'lateral thought' is intelligence, and that an intelligent person is one who is creative. We are talking, here, of that person's ability to produce links between pieces of knowledge.

Another very important part of the field of AI concerns natural language. Again, even quite retarded or sensually handicapped humans perform a remarkable process of language learning, which transcends our most complex and efficient computer systems to date. Some well known cases show that humans who are unfortunate enough to be born without the senses of sight or hearing are fully capable of learning to communicate intelligently, and use all the other faculties of the normal human being. It would appear that the intelligence of communication, though facilitated by our remarkable senses, is more an attribute of the way in which the brain is 'wired'. It is this wiring which hardware and AI workers are striving to emulate.

Natural language has probably been studied since prehistoric times, and our knowledge of language is immense. However, it is not yet sufficiently advanced to allow us to program even the largest and fastest computers to hold more than the most basic and simple conversation with a human. Again, this is not due to some restriction of the computer's senses, or its ability to communicate. It is the brain's wiring which is the problem. There is still no complete theory for the functioning of the brain.

Other areas of AI include such studies as games playing, robotics, computer vision and speech, and so on. However, probably the most compelling part of AI today remains the one of communication using natural language. You will see that micro-PROLOG is particularly well suited to this aspect of AI.

## Natural language

We are still largely conditioned to think of intelligent machines as walking talking androids, which can hold normal conversations, have total recall of facts, possess great strength, and generally surpass our frailty in many ways. Much of this comes from the large number of science fiction films which followed the great rise in popularity of science fiction stories in the first half of this century.

Science fiction provides us with an escape from the mundane constraints of normal physical laws and our lack of current knowledge on the great questions of the universe and ourselves. No writer has had as great an influence on our conception of machine intelligence as Isaac Asimov. He made the important step of bringing us a description of the robot which was scientific, and as consistent as possible. He could not, of course, explain how to build sophisticated robots, but given their existence, he tried to make their behaviour consistent, and thus opened up important issues which would otherwise have remained undiscussed until the great leap into intelligent machines had been made by science and technology. We see discussed in his stories such issues as the importance of making robots obey laws to protect humans under any circumstances. We see the interactions between humans and robots discussed, along with the internal 'emotions' of the machines. Even civil rights for robots are considered!

To some extent, these writings and the manifold offshoots from them, have given us a familiarity with intelligent machines before they can even exist. This has also shaped our exploration of AI, and one of the most important consequences is that intelligent robot communication is almost taken for granted. We now have the enormous task of coming up to that ideal.

The attribute of communication using human speech is many people's main conception of intelligence in machinery, and natural language understanding is considered by many to be the main problem of AI. It is also common to relate this problem with those of pattern recognition, speech recognition and machine vision. There is something in the structure of the brain which we are striving for, which is common to all these problems. It may be something simple which will suddenly dawn upon us; but, more likely, it is a slowly evolving study which after many years of painful work will yield little by little to allow us to build our intelligent machines.

Much of this book is concerned with aspects of natural language, and for this we need computer languages which will treat words as the basic elements, rather than numbers, or letters. We will now look at the properties of a computer language which can help in this quest.

## Sentence structure

Consider the sentence:

"Does Janet love John or Peter?"

Can you answer this question? The answer is, of course, no. The simple reason is that you do not know the relationships between the individuals involved. Furthermore, this sentence is actually two questions, plus a whole load of complex implications. For instance, are we to assume that there are only two alternatives as answers here, or are we allowed to answer that Janet loves neither John nor Peter? Perhaps there is a further individual who has received her favours, or maybe there is no one whom she loves at all? Furthermore, can we allow her the perversity of loving both, and lots more of her friends, all at the same time?

The possibilities are literally endless. We could find ourselves weighed down by a complex discussion on the meaning of love, and the true nature of Janet's feelings.

How can we begin to pick our way through the full gamut of human experience in a mechanical and computer-orientated manner to attack the meaning and generation of even the simplest general question such as the one above? The answer is that at present we cannot. We are restricted to analysing the sentence as a collection of vocabulary items, and interrogating a stored database of facts and associated rules.

The first step in analysing the above is to 'parse' the sentence. This simply means determining which words do what. For instance, we might look for the subject, verb and object of that verb in the sentence. Parsing is one of the aspects of natural language which is well covered by PROLOG. If we can understand the structure of sentences, and the positioning of different words within a sentence structure, it is a fair bet that we will be on the way to understanding how to comprehend and generate typical human sentences. We shall look at parsing as an application later in this book.

To start with, however, we will take a simpler approach, and assume that every sentence we might encounter is stylised into some standard form. This is how computer languages are defined in general, and we quickly find that even though a language such as BASIC, for instance, is not written in general human form, its few rules and structures are sufficient to express some of the most complex ideas we can imagine. Thus, one of the ways we try to circumvent the complexity of natural language is to reduce that complexity until it becomes manageable. The problem is that most human language is full of ambiguity and innuendo, and we have to rely on our experience to decipher it. In computer languages, their every utterance is clearly and uniquely defined, and there is no argument over the meaning of a BASIC sentence such as:

```
FOR N=1 TO 100: PRINT N;" SQUARED = ";N^2:NEXT N
```

For the BASIC interpreter to understand this sentence, it simply looks at the 'keyword' at the start of each statement, and interrogates its vocabulary. It is a foregone conclusion that each statement will start with a defined keyword – there are no exceptions. If you have accidentally typed in a non-keyword at the start of a statement, the computer goes no further, it reports immediately that there is an error; it does not try to work out what you really meant. This is one of the reasons for our saying that computers are stupid machines.

Unfortunately, there is no similar consistency within natural language. Natural language sentences may start with any part of speech, and may begin with the subject or the object of the main verb. They may have several levels of clause within clause, and may even leave out large quantities of vital data which are simply left as 'understood' by the reader. This is too complex to be attacked 'from the top', as it were, so we must start well below this highly complex system, and build up slowly from the bottom.

## The logic of language

We cannot hope to create intelligent programs just yet, and we must restrict ourselves to examining parts of the intelligence locked up within language. We will start by looking at the way we describe objects, and how they relate together. This is part of an important overall characteristic of intelligent natural language which we call *logic*.

When we speak, we try to be logical. We try to say things which follow a 'sensible' line. It is not easy to follow someone who darts about from statement to statement without a logical thread. We even pillory politicians and public speakers if they break this type of rule, though most of us speak much less carefully in private. However, logic is an important part of intelligence, and the AI languages try to allow logic to form an important part of their structure. In fact, micro-PROLOG is an excellent language for expressing many of the ideas of mathematical logic, though we will not concern ourselves here with this type of formalism. PROLOG, in fact, is short for *programming in logic*.

Logic in language is characterised by 'syllogisms' such as:

"George is a frog, frogs are green, therefore George is green."

This contains two bits of data – one about frogs and one about George. It then draws a third piece of data about George as a conclusion. In a certain sense this ability of the human brain to infer further facts about objects from previous experience is at the basis of our intelligence. We use language to express it, whether natural or mathematical.

Another way to think of this human activity is to liken it to an intelligent database of facts. We can think of the brain as a large storage unit of facts which come from experience. Our intelligence is able to draw those facts together, and when an external stimulus is taken in via one of our senses, it reminds us of some of those facts. When we have a problem, we appeal to our database of facts, and try to find a pattern to match the given problem to the correct answer. To do this, we may have to relate a number of database facts together in a way which we have never before considered. This is called 'lateral thought' by some people, and one's ability to use this facility is even used as the basis of IQ tests, to some extent.

An intelligent machine must be able to match up its stored facts in new ways, in some sense. This is different from simply using a filing cabinet to retrieve a piece of information. It demands that the filing cabinet itself have some internal structure for matching up its data in a way which solves a problem.

## Logic in BASIC

Let us now use a familiar computer language to look at ways of storing facts and drawing new conclusions from them. We will look for a computer program which can take in facts, store them, and then answer questions using the stored facts. In BASIC we begin by deciding how best to store the data consistently and in a form which is easily retrieved. Unfortunately, BASIC has little in the way of inherent data structures, and we would probably use arrays, which are rather better adapted to storing and manipulating numerical data, or single characters. We could start by defining a string array called DATA$. This would have to hold objects and their descriptions. For instance, we have to be able to store:

George is a frog

and

frogs are green

We can begin by extracting the essential data from these statements, and forgetting the special needs of being grammatically correct. Thus, we can reduce these two facts to:

George frog

and

frog green

In other words, let us only consider facts which consist of two words where the first is always a noun, and the second is a description of that noun – sometimes an adjective, and sometimes another noun as in the two cases here. As long as we stick to the restriction that there are only two words in the description, and the first is always described by the second, we have a consistent and uniquely retrievable system of storage.

The next question is to decide on the dimension of array DATA$, and we have already decided that it must be a string array. Suppose we were to define it as single-dimensional. We would have to store the two facts above as:

```
DATA$(1) = "George frog"
DATA$(2) = "frog green"
```

To retrieve the description of George, we would have to scan through the elements of DATA$, looking for a first word which is George. The second word in that array element would then be taken as the description. This is one of the places where BASIC lets us down, because it does not treat spaces as separators between words. There is no standard BASIC function which would return the first word in DATA$(1), for instance.

However, it is perfectly possible to construct the above, as anyone who has done some BASIC programming will know. A routine is written to look through the characters in any given string element until a space is found, then take all the letters before this space as a word, and compare it with the noun being sought. This is done for each element of DATA$ until the correct first word is found. The process then continues by looking for all the letters after the space in that element. These are then assembled into the required description word.

This is cumbersome and slow, but by no means difficult. However, a better and neater way to solve the problem is to use a 2-dimensional array, and store the facts as:

```
DATA$(1,1) = "George"
DATA$(1,2) = "frog"
DATA$(2,1) = "frog"
DATA$(2,2) = "green"
```

Thus, for each pair of elements with an equal first index, the value of the second index decides whether it is the noun or the descriptive word which is referred to. By this means, the two words of each fact are separated by more than a simple space within a string. They are stored in different array elements, and connected together by the value of the first index of DATA$.

This is a perfectly satisfactory data structure. To find the description of a given noun, a program would simply search through all the elements of DATA$ having a second index equal to 1. When the required noun is found, changing the second index to 2 will retrieve the description of that noun.

This gives some idea of the structure which must be constructed to allow

BASIC to manipulate words and sentences. The main problem is that sentences are collections of words separated by spaces, and BASIC does not recognise the space character in any special way within a string. A collection of objects separated by spaces is technically referred to as a 'list', and the manipulation of such structures is called 'list processing'. Thus, we might say that BASIC is not well adapted to list processing. To see this further, let us now look at the problem of using the data stored, and answering questions.

So far, we have looked at how to answer the cosmically crucial question:

"is George a frog?"

However, to put this query in a form which is more consistent with the above, we should write:

is"George frog" stored in DATA$ ?

We simply look at the first element of each pair, and compare it with George until equal, and then look at the second member to see if it equals frog.

But, how would we answer questions such as:

is it true that "George green"?

We know that it is true, as a consequence of the present facts, but it is not stored specifically in our array DATA$. We must allow, therefore, for questions which require inference from the facts, as well as simply checking for them to match up directly with an existing fact. We could start this by checking George green against our data stored in DATA$ as explained above. However, when it transpires that this is not in DATA$, the program would not simply give up. It would then work through the whole of DATA$ again as follows:

(a) Find the next occurrence of George in DATA$.
(b) Extract the second element (frog, say) for this occurrence.
(c) Search for frog throughout DATA$.
(d) Check the second element of frog for each find.
(e) If the second element of frog ever equals green, then give the answer TRUE then end.
(f) Go to (a).

If the process finishes without recording a TRUE value, then the answer is FALSE.

This process searches first for George, and finds frog in the second element of DATA$ for George in the first. It then searches for frog, and looks for green in the second element of which frog is the first. It will be successful here and thus gives the answer TRUE.

You can see that every step of the way we are forcing BASIC into a mould for which it was not intended. We have to set up a special data structure, we have to walk the program through the most basic fundamental parts of the logic process, and we have to construct things in such a manner that it blindly prints TRUE or FALSE at the end, without even understanding the meaning of these fundamental Boolean constants. BASIC is constructed for problems where complete descriptions, in the form of recipes, are in existence, and can be written down verbatim.

Now imagine storing sentences containing lists of more than two words to describe situations. We would have to move to higher multidimensional arrays, or produce a host of special list manipulation routines which would be stored as subroutines or procedures, and would need to be added physically to the end of each program we may write using lists. This can all be achieved in BASIC, but we would be spending too much time setting up the storage and basic tools, and not enough on the actual problems in hand. We need a new language which is adapted to storing and manipulating lists of words, and the logical relationships between them.

## Useful attributes of a new language

Any language orientated towards the tasks described above should consider word-lists as basic objects, and be able to store descriptions, and even relationships between objects so that interrogating a database of facts is easy and natural. Also, in order to allow us to interrogate a knowledge base, the language should be good at pattern matching, without having to force us to write special routines which compare each letter of each word to determine whether they are equal. Pattern matching should also be able to extend to lists of words, and thus the structure of a sentence could be checked by comparing a known pattern with a new sentence.

It is essential that we can store simple descriptive sentences in a database, and query that database as required. We shall look, now, at some facilities which would be useful in such a language.

Rather than having to define arrays, and set up the data structures from scratch, it would be useful if we could simply write in our data to the database as follows:

```
George is a frog
frogs are green
Peter is male
Janet is female
```

This is a basic set of facts about objects, but it still suffers from the problems of being rather grammatically orientated. The fact that Peter has the attribute of being a male has nothing to do with the verb "is" which is used to explain this to us. We still need to be able to make the tie-up between George and frog consistent. The trick is to consider the concept of *relations*.

## Relations

Broadly speaking, a relation is simply a method of describing an object, or binding together two or more objects. Before looking at some examples to make this clearer, we will see how relations are written down.

There are three methods of writing down relations between objects, known as 'prefix', 'postfix' and 'infix' notation. To see the difference between these forms, we will look at some familiar BASIC functions which also use these forms.

*Prefix notation* means putting the relation or function name first, followed by the arguments upon which it acts. For instance, the following is a prefix form:

```
LEFT$(X$,5)
```

Here, LEFT$ is a function whose name is always written as a prefix to the list of its arguments. It is essential that the values of the variables are placed in the brackets in the correct order, because the BASIC interpreter expects a string value in the first place, and a number in the second. If these are interposed, the system signals an error. This is true for lists of arguments of relations and functions in general.

There are other functions which are normally presented using infix notation. For instance, addition is a function of two variables, whose value is their sum. Thus:

5 + 6

is an infix method of giving the addition. In some languages and calculators, addition is given in the prefix form:

+ (5 6)

We are more used to the infix method when using the numeric operation symbols. However, there are languages which are less numerically orientated which stick to the prefix method, and use words instead of the normal numeric symbols. For instance:

SUM(X Y)

is a common method of signifying addition.

Familiar relations in BASIC are the comparison operators. For instance, the following are examples of relations written using infix notation:

| | | |
|---|---|---|
| 5 | > | 2 |
| 6 | <> | 5 |
| 3*8 | <> | 24 |

The main point is that these objects have the overall values true or false, which are part of the defining quality of a relation. A relation, broadly speaking, is a *correspondence* between two objects, which is true or false of those objects.

We have seen examples of the prefix and infix notations in BASIC, but it is a little more difficult to find postfix examples in BASIC. An example is the $ sign used to turn a numeric variable into a string variable. One might say that $ is a postfix operator which describes an identifier to the BASIC interpreter as being a string variable.

To give examples of general relations in natural language, we can think of them as being used to express something about one or more objects. For instance:

Janet loves John

is a relation between Janet and John expressed using the infix notation. It could also be written in the following manner:

loves(Janet John)

which is the prefix form. Each is equally valid and allowable, though the first is more natural to us.

It is important to remember that the order of writing the objects is crucial.

The second form above acts on a special object called a 'list'. We shall loosely define a list as a set of objects, separated by spaces, and contained within round brackets. The use of round brackets to contain lists is nearly universal.

Relations are not restricted to involving two objects, they can be defined for several objects, or just one object. The most common relations concern one and two objects, and they are called 'unary' and 'binary' relations respectively.

Examples of words which can be used as binary relations are:

```
      Janet loves John
or    loves(Janet John)

      Peter hates computers
or    hates(Peter computers)

      dog jumps stile
or    jumps(dog stile)

      trumpet member-of set-of-musical-instruments
or    member-of(trumpet set-of-musical-instruments)

      Jane plays-with daughter-of-George-and-Mary
or    plays-with(Jane daughter-of-George-and-Mary)
```

As you can see, no matter how complex the sentence, each of these examples simply has two objects, and a relation between them. Note how we make sure that no spaces are used within a given object. It is usual to bind words together to form single objects with hyphens. Remember that spaces have a very important meaning in list processing, they separate members of a list. Also, note that we keep the consistent nature of the relations by leaving out 'a' 'an' and 'the'. For instance:

the dog jumps the stile

is against the rules because now there are four objects being used with a binary relation.

Unary relations are simply used to describe single objects. For instance, some examples of words which can be used as unary relations are:

green, male, heavy, frog, an-unpleasant-person,

Some of these are adjectives, and some are nouns. Other parts of speech may also be used as unary relations. Unary relations can be presented in two forms. Prefix forms look like ordinary functions, but the postfix form is the more natural form. Examples of their use would be:

| | | |
|---|---|---|
| green(frog) | or | frog green |
| male(Peter) | or | Peter male |
| heavy(Lead) | or | Lead heavy |
| frog(George) | or | George frog |
| an-unpleasant-person(Joe) | or | Joe an-unpleasant-person |

These unary relations cannot bind one object to another, because there is only one object mentioned, hence their use as descriptions of single objects. Using these relations, we can build up a complex database on a given subject. We will do this now, and then consider how to ask it questions.

## An example of a database

Let us assume that we have a new language interpreter which automatically maintains a database of facts in the form of relations as above. We will use the more natural infix or postfix form as appropriate, and we will assume that we can add new facts to the database simply by typing them into the terminal.

Consider the problem of storing facts about the range of microcomputers on the market, and then querying the database about these facts.

We will call the computers A, B, C, D etc., and discuss attributes such as how their speeds and memory capacities compare, and the colour of their screens.

The following is a set of facts which we assume we can simply type in as shown:

```
A greater-RAM-than B
B greater-RAM-than F
A faster-than C
B faster-than A
F faster-than A
F faster-than D
B white-screen
C green-screen
D amber-screen
```

and so on.

This database of facts contains some binary relations such as faster-than, and some unary relations such as green-screen.

From this database, we would expect to be able to ask, for instance:

```
is B greater-RAM-than A?
```

and receive the answer NO. Furthermore, we would expect to be able to command:

```
list all the computers with amber screens
```

These are the natural queries which should be able to be put to a database of facts, whether machine-based, or held within a human brain. These queries are also couched in natural terms, and we should be able to put any straightforward question we can think of to the database. Questions and queries of this sort use a form of pattern matching, just as we do. It is important for the database to be able to match its data to the question, and supply the answer as a result. To see this more clearly, we will consider the latter question above in more detail.

## Variables

In BASIC, variable names are used as memory locations to store intermediate calculations. In a certain sense, we can consider those variables to contain the intermediate and final answers to the problems being processed. In BASIC, the first task is to call the answers by some names. For instance, if we wish to find the sum of three numbers, and then use that sum somewhere else, the first thing to do is to call the sum by a name such as SUM, or X etc. In the logical language we are looking at here, we will start by calling the required answer by a variable name such as X, and then construct a logical question or command including X, and hope that X is found.

For example, to list all the computers with amber screens, we start off with the command:

```
list all X such that X amber-screen
```

This puts the question in a formalised manner, and you can now look down the list of facts above, and see that the only X fitting the bill is D, which is the answer. We perform this intelligent act by a process of pattern matching. In fact, X is called the 'answer pattern' in such a command. Another example would be:

```
list all X such that X greater-RAM-than B
```

Again, if you perform your normal human type of pattern matching you will find that only the pattern A can be substituted for X.

A wider command might be:

```
list all X such that X faster-than Y
```

where Y is also a variable. If you think about this you should come to the conclusion that as X and Y can be anything, the above will involve all the 'faster-than' relations. Thus, we look at each relation in turn, and list all the Xs, i.e. all the left-hand items of the relation 'faster-than' in the database. The answer to this is:

A B F F

Note that the second occurrence of F in the answer pattern is printed here on the assumption that the process of pattern matching is performed blindly and literally in a sequence.

The use of variables as answer patterns is probably quite near to our human method of looking at this type of problem. We tend to keep in our 'mind's eye' a pattern for which we are looking in a list of items, and when the pattern matches, we have the answer. This type of facility in a computer language is very powerful, as we shall see.

Another human trait is to take existing relations, and combine them into further relations. We will look at this next.

## Manipulation of relations

It would be useful to be able to combine and alter relations, and thus produce new ones. For instance, if we wanted a relation between computers which was the reverse of faster-than, i.e. slower-than, we could build it up by reversing faster-than. We would want, therefore, to be able to write new relations in terms of old ones. For instance, a human would say:

```
X slower-than Y if Y faster-than X
```

This is a perfectly good definition which we could give to anyone. Similarly, we could define 'smaller-RAM-than' using:

```
X smaller-RAM-than Y if Y greater-RAM-than X
```

In exactly the same way that the facts could be added to the database by typing them in, we would expect to be able to add these new relation definitions, or rules, to the database, and thus effectively extend it considerably without, for instance, explicitly defining slower-than for each appropriate pair of computers involved. This is an example of automatic inference.

If we wish to build up larger relations, then we need Boolean operations such as 'and'. For instance, if we were to define the relation 'better-than' as meaning faster and with greater RAM, then we could define this relation using:

```
X better-than Y if
X faster-than Y  and  X greater-RAM-than Y
```

As you can see, these operations are instantly recognisable from our normal experience of natural language. If our new computer language can cater for this type of structure, it will be well adapted to natural language. However, you should not lose sight of the fact that all this is still possible in BASIC, but it is simply not as easy.

Another important subject is that of data structures, and one of the favourites is the 'tree' structure. We will look at how this is included in normal language next.

## Data structures

A data structure is just a method of storing data. BASIC has several data structures, but none of them is suitable for our purposes, without modification. For instance, the DATA statement stores data in a straightforward linear form where the data items are available in a simple sequence. The array, as we have seen, is useful for storing data which is to be retrieved by using an index. Other data structures, such as data trees, have to be manufactured using arrays in BASIC.

In natural language, we are constantly using data trees without noticing it. They suggest a hierarchy to the knowledge which we possess. For instance, the following is a tree of data:

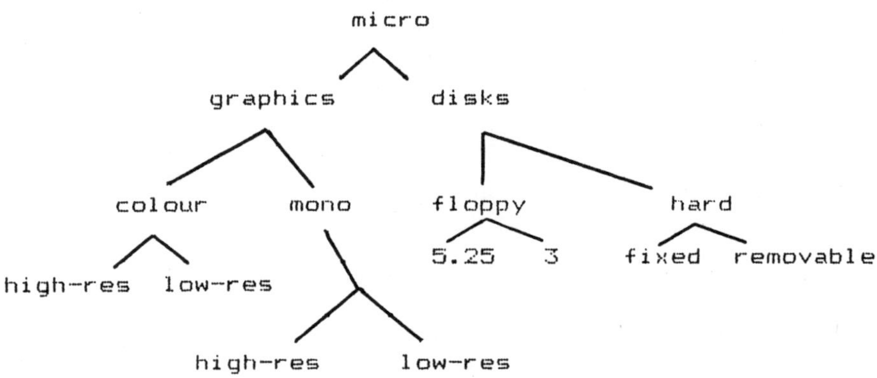


This simply shows a tree of microcomputer attributes, and might form the basis of a check list reminder of the type of questions to ask when buying a computer. The data is stored in a hierarchical form, and could be retrieved from the top by asking simple yes/no questions, and following the appropriate branch at each stage. For instance, the first question might be about the graphics – does it have colour or not? In this simple tree, either answer leads onto the same next question. After this has been attended to, the user would retreat to the top of the tree again, and take the other branch and ask questions about the disks.

The form of the data structure itself suggests the type of program which will use it. However, it is not easy to input and use data in this two-dimensional form within a computer – data is better input as a sequential set of items. The tree above can also be represented in a one-dimensional form as a list of items which are linked together in the same way as above. This is called a 'linked list', which provides one of the most important uses of relations. They can be used to link data together into a structured list. It does not have to be a simple tree as above; it could be a network, or a many-branched tree, for instance. We will now look at how we would use relations to store the tree above.

The trick is to think of how you would store the data in your head – i.e. how would you memorise the data? The answer is that you would convert the data into words, using relations. For instance, you would say:

    the micro uses graphics

or

    the micro has disks

and so on. We can do a similar thing in computing, but we cannot assume the subtlety of understanding of the human brain. For instance, the two sentences above use different relations, but we know that they come to the same thing, though they have different connotations and deeper meanings. We have to make our computer relations rather crude and simple. Thus, we would rewrite the above two sentences to use the same relation, and even insist on spelling it the same way. In fact, we could have several different spellings of a given relation, to allow tenses etc., but we would have to add in a definition to tell the computer to regard them the same way.

The two sentences could thus be written as:

    micro contains graphics

and

    micro contains disks

This makes the first relation required at the top of the tree consistent.

The rest of the tree is stored in a similar manner, again standardising the relations involved. The result might be as follows:

```
micro contains graphics
micro contains disks
graphics type-is colour
graphics type-is mono
colour type-is high-res
colour type-is low-res
mono type-is high-res
```

mono type-is low-res
disks type-is floppy
disks type-is hard
floppy type-is 5.25
floppy type-is 3
hard type-is fixed
hard type-is removable

This stores the complete tree such that each item is linked to the one below, as shown in the tree.

We can move through the tree by asking questions of the relation 'type-is'. For instance, to see the ends of the branches from the word 'mono', we could simply ask:

list all X such that mono type-is X

This would give high-res and low-res as expected.

The whole tree has thus been represented by a linked list of simple sentences. Each sentence is a fact in its own right, but overlaps with one or more of the other facts in the list. In this way, a complete database of information can be stored and retrieved on any subject. The method involved is very human-orientated, and can produce the type of user-friendly programs which AI is continually seeking.

## Conclusion

When we talk we use a form of logic all the time. To reproduce and comprehend our natural languages, we need a computer language which can be used to manipulate the type of logical sentences which we understand. This naturally leads us away from the so called 'imperative' languages such as BASIC, and into a new form of computer language where we can define relations between objects in our experience, and descriptions of those objects.

Communication is a means of using lists of words, where each word has a meaning, and a place within the sentence. Understanding is a question of matching patterns to that communication. A small child learns to perform this trick over a period of several years, and he then has a uniquely complex system for building further, and creating new ideas. Machines can be made to participate in communication, and the problem is made considerably easier by choosing the correct language for that communication.

## Summary

**(a)** A *database* is a set of items of information stored in a standardised form. An expert system uses a database, which is referred to as a *knowledge base*.

**(b)** *Communication* is at the basis of AI, and thus an *AI-orientated language* should be able to deal with *words*.

**(c)** A *list* is a set of objects separated by spaces, and normally written within round brackets.

**(d)** A *relation* binds two or more objects together, or describes single objects. The latter are called *unary relations*, and the former *binary relations* when referring to two objects.

**(e)** A database of facts may be used to store a *tree* of data. These facts are simply sentences using relations to describe words.

**(f)** When querying a database, variables are used to provide an *answer pattern* for which the query is searching. For instance, to translate the question:

which micros are faster than the micro A

we would write:

list all X such that X faster-than A

X is called the answer pattern, and it is found by searching through the stored database of facts for any X which satisfies the sentence above.

# Chapter Two
# Introduction to SIMPLE and micro-PROLOG

## Introduction

The last chapter introduced some of the basic concepts which micro-PROLOG relies upon, and this chapter introduces the language itself. micro-PROLOG comes with a package of special modules and 'front-end processors'. One of these is called SIMPLE, and it makes programming in micro-PROLOG somewhat easier than using the general form of the language. We shall look at this form first, and describe the general form later in the book. The general form of micro-PROLOG is called 'base code' or 'standard syntax'. SIMPLE allows the concepts of logical programming to be assimilated without the more complex ideas of the language making the task more difficult. It is straightforward to progress to base code later.

We shall rely heavily on examples which use words and language, and much of the language is best understood by remembering that it is strictly logical. You should be able to resolve most problems which you may have with the language by applying natural logic.

micro-PROLOG comes in a number of forms for different machines, and this book is written to apply to any form of the language on any machine. As a consequence, you should be ready to consult your version's manual whenever you come upon a problem or the screen shows an error. In addition, there are several facilites which are necessarily machine-dependent – for instance, editing on the screen, or storage of programs.

The chapters in this book contain numbered examples throughout, and answers to these examples appear at the end of the chapter.

## Data types

micro-PROLOG can act on a number of different types of object, and we shall look at these now.

The main objects to be manipulated are words, and these are represented by alphanumeric strings, containing no spaces, and starting with a letter. They may also contain hyphens instead of spaces as we saw in the last chapter. Also, case (upper- or lower-case) is important. For instance, Frog and frog are considered to be different words. The following are alphanumeric constants:

frog
faster-than
green
This-is-a-constant
H212

As you can see, a relation name, such as faster-than, is simply a normal constant which is used in a special way. We will see this shortly.

Another type of constant is the numeric constant. micro-PROLOG allows numbers to be used with or without signs, and with or without decimal points. The following are numeric constants:

13
−54
−324.678

We will see how micro-PROLOG treats numbers later. For now we will concentrate on words.

Another form of constant which is allowed in micro-PROLOG is the quoted constant. We will see that some alphanumeric objects are automatically taken to be variables in micro-PROLOG, and to change one of these to a constant, it should be placed within double quotes. You should consult your manual to confirm the exact form of this type of constant. You will see that this is rarely needed, as the variables are chosen to be rather different from any normal words which we might use.

Variables in micro-PROLOG are simply the letters:

x y z X Y Z

as well as any alphanumeric string made up of one of these followed by an integer. Thus the following are also automatically treated as variables:

x1 x2 X3 z53 Y79

Note that the integer is treated numerically in that the variables x24 and x0024 are the same variable because they use equal integers.

The other type of object which micro-PROLOG uses is the list. We will see some powerful list manipulation facilites later in the book. A list is a collection of objects written between round brackets. The following are examples of lists:

(the cat sat on the mat)
(A faster-than B)
(This is a list (and this is a sublist))

The first list contains six members, and the second three, each of which is an alphanumeric constant. The third list contains five members, one of which is a 'sublist' containing five alphanumeric constants. This hierarchy of lists and sublists is very important in list processing, and we shall return to it later in the book.

## Relations

Relation names can be alphanumeric constants, and it is important to ensure that when a relation is used or defined it is not confused with the objects it is acting upon.

We have seen how relations such as:

A faster-than B

are defined using infix notation. This is a very natural and understandable way of writing relations, but it can only work properly for binary relations. Consider the more complex relation:

Peter takes Mary to Spain

This involves three main objects, and relates them together in a straightforward manner. However, it is not so easy for the machine to work out which of the five words here is the relation. Normally, we would expect the machine to do it by the positioning of each word within the sentence. However, we might have written the sentence as:

to Spain Peter takes Mary

It is not surprising that we have to use a standardised form of such relations. A relation which has three arguments is called a 'ternary' relation, and the general form uses prefix notation. Thus the above sentence is written:

takes(Peter Mary Spain)

The order of objects within the argument is crucial; once chosen it must be adhered to religiously. Here, the object doing the taking is placed in the first position, the object being taken in the second, and the destination in the third.

Thus, ternary (and higher order) relations must always be entered in the prefix form as shown. Binary and unary relations, which are the most common relations, are allowed their special infix and postfix forms in SIMPLE as a concession to readability.

## A micro-PROLOG session

micro-PROLOG does not have line-numbers in order to store its programs and data. The commands and questions you type into the computer are executed immediately, and they may be transient, or affect the storage of data, or of the program being assembled at the time. You will see how to do this shortly. For the moment, let us see how to set the language up for a session.

All language interpreters have a system prompt, and the cursor starts by sitting next to that prompt, waiting for you to start typing. In micro-PROLOG, the prompt is an ampersand sign followed by a full-stop. Thus, when you first load micro-PROLOG, you will find that the cursor is sitting next to a prompt which looks like this:

```
&.
```

If you now press a few random keys, followed as always by RETURN, or ENTER, etc., depending upon your particular machine, you will probably find that micro-PROLOG signifies its displeasure at the rubbish it has just been given by signalling an error. This will show that the language has loaded properly.

In order to follow this chapter on your computer, you should now load the SIMPLE module. This can normally be done by the following:

```
&LOAD SIMPLE
```

using upper-case throughout. Note that the the letter L has replaced the full-stop after the & sign. You should refer to your manual to see how to load SIMPLE to ensure that you have loaded the correct disk or tape, etc. SIMPLE takes a fair time to load, even from disk, and you should not become impatient too soon! Also, SIMPLE takes up a large amount of space, and if you can maximise the amount of space available for the system, you should do this before loading.

Once it has loaded, SIMPLE uses lower-case almost entirely, so you should ensure that your CAPS LOCK is switched off. You will find that this matter of case is one of the more common means of causing an error, and you should take notice of the case of any command before using it. This will be emphasised as necessary below.

When SIMPLE has finished loading, the &. prompt will reappear, and you are ready to go. We will start with an activity which is at the basis of most of the work you will do with micro-PROLOG.

## Setting up a database

Before we can look at micro-PROLOG programming, the basic keywords of SIMPLE must be introduced. Some of these are specifically for setting up and maintaining the internal database. They are introduced in this section.

Setting up a database in micro-PROLOG is performed exactly as explained in the last chapter. The relations, and facts about the objects involved, are simply typed in verbatim, according to a few standard rules. You can also inspect the database using a special list function, and members of the database can be altered, deleted, or placed in any position within the structure. We will now look at the special keywords used in micro-PROLOG for playing with databases.

These keywords are:

add accept list delete edit kill

Note that these are all in lower-case. They allow a database of simple sentences (relations) to be placed in store. You must think of a special area of memory being set aside for a single database, which is maintained during your session with the computer. You are allowed to save the database, and load it back again at a later date to allow you to continue where you left off. As you will find out, this database stores more than a few basic facts for your program to access later; the database actually stores the program itself. The program is stored as a set of relations and commands within the database. We shall see this as we progress through the language.

## add and accept

The add keyword is used to add new sentences to the database, either onto the end of the database, or into any position within the database. The accept keyword is also used to add to the database, and allows a string of new members to be added without having to type in 'add' each time. We will use add and accept to create a database from scratch, and then add some further facts at various different positions. If you are following this on a computer, you should type the examples below into the machine as you are reading through.

To start the database off, let us place a single binary relation onto it. Type in:

```
add(A faster-than B)
```

As you can see, the add function acts upon a list which contains a relation. This form must be adhered to accurately, except that the relation within the list's brackets can be any allowable relation. To ensure that you always remember to use as many right brackets as left, the machine checks as it goes. If you miss out a right bracket, and press RETURN, the & prompt is replaced with a 1. instead. This tells you that one level of brackets is missing. In later work, where several levels of brackets will be needed, it is easy to miss a closing bracket or two, and this facility reminds you to add them in. Try leaving out the right bracket in the next input, and then add it in when asked for it by the 1. Type in the following:

```
add(frog green)
```

and

```
add(takes(Peter Mary Spain))
```

When you have typed these into the machine, the complete database can be viewed by typing:

```
list all
```

This will print out the relations above, without the list brackets, or the add keyword. The display will show:

```
A faster-than B
frog green
takes (Peter Mary Spain)
```

In general, the infix and postfix form will be used wherever possible, for readability, and otherwise the prefix form will be used. Thus, if you were to type in:

```
add(blue(water))
```

meaning that you are describing water as blue, then when you list it, the database will display it as:

```
water blue
```

The same holds for binary relations, which are also acceptable in prefix form if you wish. In the underlying 'standard synatax' form of the language, all relations are presented in a prefix form.

To see where the database stores new data, try typing in:

```
add(D faster-than E)
list all
```

You will see that micro-PROLOG has stored this latest example of faster-than next to the last use of this relation in the database. If you now add:

```
add(grass green)
list all
```

The display should show:

```
A faster-than B
D faster-than E
frog green
grass green
takes (Peter Mary Spain)
water blue
```

As you add further examples for a given relation, they are stored at the end of the current list of entries for that relation within the database.

The add keyword can take an optional number to define the position of the new member within the area containing that relation. For instance, if you wish to add a further member of the green relation, between frog green and grass green, simply use the number 2 in the add function to denote that it is to be added in the second position within the green data. The following achieves this:

```
add 2 (paint green)
```

It is important to remember that the position denoted here is the position within the green members, and not the position in the overall database. This effectively means that the database is sectionalised into separate areas, one for each relation.

If we now wished to add in the data within the tree of the last chapter, it would take some time to use add for each member of the type-is relation. The keyword 'accept' comes in useful here. If 'accept' is typed in, followed by the relation to be added to, only the new members need to be typed in from then on. We will now input all the type-is relations within the tree. You will have to refer continually to the tree diagram below. Try to tie up the database structure with that of the diagram for the tree throughout. Type in:

```
accept type-is
```

This will cause the normal & prompt to be replaced by type-is, followed by a full-stop. From now on, any list of two items which you type in will be added to the type-is relation in the database. The process is terminated by typing in the word 'end'. Look at the previous chapter and type in all the entries as follows (do not type in the type-is itself – that will be supplied by the machine):

```
type-is(graphics colour)
type-is(graphics mono)
type-is(colour high-res)
      .
      .
      .
      .
type-isend
&.
```

You now have a useful database containing a number of relations, and several members per relation. To complete the tree you will have to add in a couple of further members for the 'contains' relation. You should do this now, using add or accept.

It is important to keep in mind the positions within the database at which data is stored. This is particularly useful when we come to querying the database. Querying occurs from the top down, in general, and knowing this can help you to write programs more efficiently.

## list

We have seen how to list the whole database, using list all, but as it increases, it becomes impossible to pick out the data within a given area by this means.

However, you can list a given relation if you wish, by typing in the relation name after the word list. Try the following:

```
list green
```

The members of that relation will appear on the screen.

When adding new data, there is no reason why you should not repeat the same items, and to see this, type in the following:

```
add(frog green)
list green
```

You will see that this has been added at the end of the green members, even though it is a repeat of a previous item. micro-PROLOG does not check what you are adding to the database, except syntactically.

The list function helps you to retain an idea of the way in which your database is being stored.

## delete and kill

If you now wish to delete the second occurrence of the frog green member, you can use 'delete'. Again, the specific sentence to be deleted can be typed in, in which case only the first occurrence of that sentence will be removed. Alternatively, a relation name and a number can be used to select a specific member for deletion, if you know where it is.

To delete the second occurrence of frog green, type in:

```
delete green 4
```

because the required member is the fourth item in the green list. Note that the number appears at the end, unlike for add where it appears immediately after the add.

To use the other form of the delete keyword, type in:

```
delete(frog green)
```

This is used exactly as for add, and will remove the first occurrence of the given sentence, which at this point will be the only occurrence.

Now recreate the green list using accept – there will be four members which describe frog, paint, grass and frog in that order. Now list green to ensure that the base is correct.

An entire relation, with all of its members, can be removed from the database using the kill command. Simply follow the word kill with the relation name. Try:

```
kill green
list all
```

You will find that all the entries for the green relation have been removed.

The entire database can be deleted by using kill all, but this should only be done after the current database has been stored as described later. When using kill all, you will have to answer a question which ensures that you really mean to kill everything, which is displayed as a warning of this extreme command.

**edit**

The exact use of this function depends upon your particular machine, though all machines will be broadly the same. To change some aspect of one of the database members, you will have to know its position within its particular area. For instance, the fifth member of the type-is relation should be:

```
mono type-is high-res
```

any part of this can be changed, including both the position of the member within the relation, and even the relation itself. If the relation is changed, then the position number automatically refers to the position within the new relation's area.

To edit this item, type in:

```
edit type-is 5
```

The machine should reply with something like:

```
5 (mono type-is high-res)
```

You can now either retype the whole line, or use the correction facilities of your machine, to change the 5 to a 1, for example, and then list the relation to see that this member has moved to the first place.

Before continuing, you should move this member back into the fifth position, for future use.

Now try the following:

```
edit blue 1
```

This should display:

```
1 (water blue)
```

Now use your normal editing procedure to change this to:

```
1 (water green)
```

and list the green relation. If you have been following the examples so far, then the green relation will have been killed off in the previous section, and water green will be the only relation in that category now. If you still have some green members from before, then this new member will have been put in first place, pushing all the others down one place as a result. This action does not delete the previous member in that position, it simply shifts it down.

By using edit, you can alter the database in a variety of ways, and we shall look at some examples shortly.

## dict

Every relation name which micro-PROLOG refers to in its database is placed on a separate file called the dictionary, or dict for short. This list of words is used by SIMPLE as a reference for such actions as listing the members of a database. You can view the names stored on the dict by typing in:

```
list dict
```

You should see all the familiar names of relations involved in the current database stored there. Each of these names is followed by the word 'dict' to emphasise that it is stored on the dictionary, and the word dict is thus simply treated as a type of unary relation, used in the postfix form.

It is also possible to add and delete dict members, exactly as for any other unary relation. For instance:

```
delete dict 5
```

will remove the fifth member of the dict list, and the following:

```
delete(faster-than dict)
```

will remove the faster-than entry on the dict. If list all, or list for the given relation above, is typed in, these two relations will be missing. However, the dict is only a reference, and just as when you lose the index to a book, the data still remains within the pages, so the data is still in the database after the dict entry has been removed. To see this, you can add the reference back again as follows:

```
add(faster-than dict)
```

just as for an ordinary relation. Now the list function will bring the data back for that relation as if nothing has happened. However, if you now list all, the whole database is listed as normal, but the dict items are also listed, along with the new entry:

```
dict dict
```

This is because you have played around with the word dict as if it were a relation, and this has resulted in dict being placed on the dictionary as an entry. This then references the dict itself when the whole database is listed. To reverse this new list format, simply delete the 'dict dict' entry, and the whole structure returns to normal.

The dict is not normally regarded as an ordinary unary relation within the database; it is in a list apart, and is effectively a unary relation of other relations. However, as you can see, you can also regard dict as simply a relation within part of the database for which there is no entry within the dictionary, until you force one to be put there as above.

The next section shows you how important the dict is in loading and saving information in micro-PROLOG.

## load and save

Again, these facilities are dependent upon your machine, and whether you are using disk, tape or microcartridge. The words which apply are load and save, in lower-case. If you have followed the examples so far, you should have the tree of data stored in the computer, along with some other relations. The tree has only two relations: contains and type-is. To save this tree without the other relations, we will use save after removing the other relations first. However, you may want to keep the whole current database for later, so we will store two files. One will contain the exact state of the database at present, and the other will be just the tree.

First, use save as follows to save the current data onto a file called state1:

```
save state1
```

This should save the data. Now list all to remind yourself of what is stored, and remove all the unwanted data. Remember, you can remove things either by sentence or by position using delete, or you can kill whole relations using kill. For instance:

```
kill takes
kill faster-than
kill green
```

will probably remove most of the unwanted data, though that data will still be available when you need it in the file called state1. Finish off by checking through the remaining data to ensure that there are no unwanted items. The tree data should have two 'contains' members, and 12 'type-is' members.

Once you have isolated the tree data, it should be stored as a file called tree:

```
save tree
```

We will use this again later.

To see how load works, use kill all to clear the database, and load tree. This brings in the 14 database items. Now, load tree a second time, and list just the contains relation. You will see that there are four items there instead of just two. The load function simply adds to the existing database, without removing the previous contents. This can be used to store parts of a final program, and load back just those bits you require for any given application.

There is a further complication, concerned with the dict. To see this, try a list all, and you will see that this prints four copies of the data loaded in, instead of two as you should expect. The reason for this is that the dict contains two copies of all the dict items, one for each load, and the database itself contains two copies of the database items for the same reason. Thus, as the list all function proceeds, it runs through the first half of the new dict, printing the two copies of the initial database, and then runs through the second half of the dict repeating the whole process.

The main reason for this strange behaviour is that we have performed the somewhat eccentric action of double loading a file. If you load two completely different files, then the problem does not arise. However, if you load two overlapping files, then the effect will be seen again on the overlapping items. As far as the database and all its uses are concerned, there is only the amount of data you would expect, but the dict contains too much data. The best answer, if this turns out to be a problem after a load, is carefully to delete the extra unwanted dict items.

*Example 2.1*

Start off with a clean slate by kill all, before attempting the following on a computer.

(a) Input the following data using accept, and add, as appropriate. Remember to terminate the accept using the word 'end', without brackets.

```
A before B
B before C
C before D
D before E
E before F
X after W
```

Using edit, move 'C before D' to the end of the 'before' relation base, and then change the first item above to 'B after A', and place it at the end of the database. How could you store just the resulting 'after' part of the database onto a file called 'after1', and the 'before' part onto a separate file called 'before1'? You will probably find that you cannot create a file with the same name as any existing defined word, hence the use of the 1 postscript here.

If you kill all, now, and load the 'after1' file followed by the 'before1' file, what would you expect to see displayed by 'list all'? When you have written down the answer, do it using the machine.

(b) Using the result of the last part of (a), delete every other 'before' sentence, starting at the top, using delete, and calling the items up by position number. Use list all at this point to check on your actions. If you have succeeded, you should only have members left which refer to D E and C D. If this is not the case, start from scratch and try again. You may find that this is trickier than it looks!

Having done this, add the following members using add followed by a number and the relation name as indicated:

```
H before I     in the first position
I before J     in the third position
```

Can you write down the resulting database before listing it? This will show whether you are keeping mental track of the state of the database as you create it. This becomes too great a task as the base increases, but some attempt should always be made to know the main attributes of the data when using the database. This can help to make your programs more efficient.

(c) Create a new ternary relation called 'paints', and make up a database of facts about this relation from the text below:

*Mary paints an oil of a lamb, and Peter is busy painting the hills in water colour. While these two are working there is a famous artist over the hedge painting the sky in oils, which itself paints a vast vista across the heavens in cloud.*

As a clue, there should be four entries for this relation. Are you forced to use a particular notation for the relation's data, or can you use more than one form?

### Queries

The commands introduced so far allow a database to be set up, added to, amended and stored. The next stage is to learn how to retrieve data from the database in an intelligent manner. In other words, we need to discover how to query the database.

The reason for creating the above databases is to allow the data stored there to be interrogated for its content by the user, or by a program. We will now look at the SIMPLE keywords which are available for querying a database. To follow this, you should kill the current contents of memory, and load in the tree file, or type it in from scratch. This will be used in examples.

There are four query keywords:

is    all    which    one

and a number of subsidiary words and symbols which help to make the queries more sophisticated:

and (or &)    or    :    if    defined    reserved    dict

### is, all and which

There are several types of question and command which would normally be asked of a database. For instance, it may be of use to know whether a particular piece of data is present, or to list out all the occurrences of a given type of fact. Other important questions concern the set of facts which satisfy a given set of conditions. For instance, in a database of facts about a set of crimes, it may be important for a police officer to know which burglary crimes are on file. Similarly, if one has a large tree of data stored about the different types of microcomputers available, it may be useful to select a set of makes which satisfy the criteria of a customer looking for a specific type of machine. These are simple queries about a database, and all of them, along with many more types, can be catered for using the few keywords given above.

To tell whether a given member is present, the is query is used. For instance, if you have loaded in the microcomputer tree, you should be able to type in the following and receive a positive answer:

```
is(mono type-is low-res)
```

The correct answer is YES, because the list above contains a member of the database. The computer will print out:

```
YES
&.
```

If you now look for a member which is not present, for instance:

```
is(a type-is b)
```

the answer is:

```
NO
&.
```

If, instead, you look for a relation whose name is not even defined, micro-PROLOG informs you of its lack of definition by giving an error. This occurs by typing in the following:

```
is(a b c)
```

Can you see what the machine is trying to make of this? The answer is that it assumes the list here contains a binary relation called 'b', because the list has three members. If the list contained two members, the interpreter would assume that the second member was a unary relation, and again would give an error of a similar kind.

We can now check for the presence of a specific data base member, but we do not always want to be so specific. For instance, suppose that we simply wanted to know that there was some information on the subject of disks in the database, but we were not interested in the specific items involved. Following the use of variables in the last chapter, we might ask a question such as: 'is there a relation present of the form "disks type-is X" where X is anything'? This is exactly the form of a general 'is' query as follows:

```
is(disks type-is X)
```

We have used one of the standard variables defined at the start of the chapter. The answer to this question is also YES, as there is at least one member of this form in the database. If the question had been asked with X and disks transposed, the answer would have been NO because there is no member of the type-is relation with the word disks as its second argument. Thus we can ask the same general questions, by using variables, as we would in some forms of ordinary parlance.

We can go further with variables in the query above and use variables for both arguments of the relation name. This can cause an interesting condition to arise, and the following examples are useful for pointing this out.

If we were simply interested to know whether type-is is represented in the database, one way to find out would be to ask a question of the form: 'Is there a member of the form "something type-is something"?'. In other words, using a variable for both places in the relation will allow any of the members to give an affirmative, if there is at least one member of this form present. What would you consider to be the result of the following?

```
is(X type-is X)
```

The answer comes from applying strict logic to the pattern in the list, and deciding whether such a member is present in the database. Correct logic would be to say that the pattern within the list above is only satisfied by a member having the same object in each of its arguments, because the same variable has been used in each place. There is no member of this form in the database, and the result is NO. The following, however, has the answer YES:

```
is(X type-is Y)
```

because it is satisfied by any member of the type-is database.

The use of variables is even more important for the keyword 'all'. This keyword will print out all the members of a database satisfying the conditions of a query placed in a list after the keyword. Again, the form of the conditional sentence is a familiar one in normal speech. It represents commands such as: 'print out all the objects in the database such that something type-is low-res'. If you look at the tree diagram, or the database, you see that there are two objects which satisfy this condition. The objects are colour and mono. Transforming this command into micro-PROLOG form, we might write:

```
all(X such that X type-is low-res)
```

This is not quite right as the 'such that' in micro-PROLOG is represented by a colon. The correct form is:

```
all(X : X type-is low-res)
```

which is much neater and easier to type anyway. The part of the list before the colon is called the 'answer pattern', and the part after the colon is called the 'query condition'.

As mentioned above, the answers to this are:

```
colour
mono
No (more) answers
&.
```

The last sentence shown is micro-PROLOG's way of assuring you that it has finished looking right through the database, comparing the answer pattern with the database entries according to the query condition. This is exactly how the job is done, and you should bear this in mind when you use queries.

*Example 2.2*

Write out the answers to the following queries before trying them out, or looking at the end of this chapter for the answers:

(a) is (micro contains Y)
(b) is (X contains X)
(c) all (X:X contains disks)
(d) all (X:X contains X)
(e) all (X:X contains Y)

Note that the 'word' which is exactly equivalent to 'all', and may thus replace it everywhere in the above. The two are interchangeable. For instance, the following prints out the entire type-is database:

```
which(X:X type-is Y)
```

which (and all) have other useful attributes. They can take comments, as well as multi-arguments in the answer pattern before the colon. For instance, in the last command, we could have put X and Y before the colon, with a message:

```
which(objects are X and Y:X type-is Y)
```

or

```
all(objects are X and Y:X type-is Y)
```

The message items are ignored, but printed out verbatim, and the variables are set to the answers sequentially, and printed out as the process proceeds. Look at the database, and you will see that the above gives the following:

```
objects are graphics and colour
objects are graphics and mono
objects are colour and high-res
      .
      .
      .
      .
      .
```

and so on.

The use of comments to be printed verbatim is useful in making program output more intelligible.

## Conjunctive conditions

To construct more complex query conditions, in order to search for data more selectively, simple conditional sentences can be combined using 'and'. A rather artificial, but instructive example of this would be to print out all the objects which are types of disk, and which can be described as fixed. We would have to combine these two conditions using an 'and', exactly as we have done automatically in the last sentence. Look at the tree, and see if you can write down all the objects which satisfy these conditions. Then type in the following, and see if you were right:

```
which(object is X:disks type-is X and X type-is fixed)
```

In other words, find all the occurrences of X such that X is a type of disk, and X is fixed. The only answer is 'hard'. This answer could have been produced, of course, by asking:

```
which(X:X type-is fixed)
```

However, this is only possible because you already know what is contained within the database. If the database were unknown, the conjunctive query condition above would be a reasonable way of asking the question.

Conjunctive conditions can also be used in an 'is' query. The one above could be written, for instance:

```
is(disks type-is X and X type-is fixed)
```

The answer which will appear will be YES signifying that there is at least one such X in the database.

Note that one of the most common sources of mistakes is to forget the colon in a which or all, and to put it in unnecessarily in an 'is' query. Either of these will cause an error to be signalled by the interpreter.

The 'and' in the conjunctive condition can be replaced with an ampersand, which makes typing easier. Thus the last query could have been written:

```
is(disks type-is X & X type-is fixed)
```

Ampersand will be used exclusively from now on, for neatness.

The query condition, in all the commands above, can have more that two sentences joined together with &. Thus the following:

```
all(X:X type-is low-res & X type-is high-res &
        graphics type-is X)
```

has answers:

```
colour
mono
```

This is a rather long-winded method of defining these two objects, but it shows the principle. There is no defined upper limit to the size of the query condition.

### one

The 'one' keyword is a way of forcing the which query to proceed at the pace of the user. This query searches for the first occurrence of the answer pattern, displays it, and then asks whether to continue. Try typing in:

```
one(X:X type-is Y)
```

The first answer is displayed on the screen, and then a question is asked as to whether to continue. If you answer in the affirmative, the next answer is displayed, and this continues until you give a negative answer.

This query is a useful way of simply looking at a few answers to a question which may have too many answers for the user to assimilate at one time.

The use of multi-variable answer patterns, messages and conjunctions are exactly as for the previous query keywords.

### Evaluation method for queries

In logical programming, it is often crucial to know both the order of evaluation of the commands, and the method of evaluation. This leads to some of the more complex concepts within micro-PROLOG, and the following examples show these concepts at work.

Consider the query:

```
all(X:X type-is fixed)
```

During evaluation, the interpreter works through the entire database, from the top down, looking for any members which have this form, with the word 'fixed' on the right-hand side of a type-is relation. The left-hand side is then printed out. The whole database is searched so that no possible occurrences will be missed.

Now consider the example:

```
is(X type-is fixed & X type-is removable)
```

Here, the database is searched from the top for a sentence matching up with the first part of the query condition. When it finds one, it transfers the value of X in that sentence to the second part of the query, and searches the whole database for any occurrence of this new sentence. If one is found, YES is printed and the process finishes. If one is not found, the search continues for the next X satisfying the first part of the query. This double search process is repeated until YES results, or it runs out of data, in which case NO is printed. This double search, one within the other, is similar to 'nested FOR loops' in BASIC.

The ramifications of this search method can be seen in a characteristic example. In the tree, some objects appear at the end of more than one branch in the structure. For instance, there are two branches having high-res at their ends, while there is only one branch leading to fixed. Consider the following query:

```
all(X:Y type-is X & Z type-is X)
```

What do you think the answer will be? To answer this question, you will have to look at the tree, or inspect the database. If you religiously search through the database, finding values for Y and X, in the first part of the query, and then transfer X to the second part, and search through the whole tree again, you will certainly find the correct answers. The question is, will this show up those objects having just two branches pointing to them, or not?

It appears at first glance that this query will ask for just those objects which have two distinct branches pointing to them – one for Y and one for Z for all pairs Y Z. However, the logical answer depends upon the meaning of 'for all' in the last sentence. In general this includes the case where Y and Z are equal. For instance, in the query above, Y and Z could be 'hard', and X could be 'fixed'. This satisfies the query condition, and thus fixed will be printed along with all the other members of the type-is relation except for graphics and disks. Using different variables does not ensure that those objects will be distinct in the search.

The answer will be something like:

```
colour
mono
high-res
high-res
low-res
low-res
high-res
high-res
low-res
low-res
floppy
hard
5.25
3
fixed
removable
```

Can you see why this is before continuing? You should list the type-is relation, because the exact order of the above depends upon the order of the database members.

The process starts by finding any Y and X in the type-is relation, in that order. If you have:

```
graphics type-is colour
```

as the first member of your type-is relation, then Y equals graphics, and X equals colour at the start. This gives a potential answer for X, as required. The value of X thus found is transferred to the second part of the query, and the database searched for a Z such that:

```
Z type-is colour
```

There is one at the very start of the database, and thus colour is an answer for X, and it is printed. However, this is not the end of the search for a Z, and the rest of the database is combed for another pattern satisfying the above. None occurs, and the process ends there. Again, the first part of the query is used to search further down the database, and mono is found in the same way.

When the search reaches the point where X equals high-res, Y is set equal to colour, and there are two cases where:

```
Z type-is high-res
```

They are for Z equals colour, and Z equals mono. Both of these give a print for X, and hence two high-res answers appear together. The same occurs for low-res, and then X equals high-res again for Y equals mono this time.

The rest of the printout will be obvious to you if you have followed the above description. To understand some of the strange outputs which micro-PROLOG gives, you will have to master the method of evaluation. The more queries, or conditions which are proceeding at once, the more nested loops there will be to follow.

*Example 2.3*
Input the following database:

```
Mary likes Pam
Mary likes Jack
Mary likes Paul
Pam likes Sue
Sue likes George
Pam likes Harry
Jack likes Harry
Mary hates George
Mary hates Harry
```

(a) Construct an 'is' query to confirm that George does not specifically like anyone.

(b) Mary now decides to have a party. She starts by inviting just the people she specifically likes. Construct a query to display her first guest list.

(c) Mary then has misgivings about leaving out her friends' friends, even if she hates them. Construct a query for the rest of the guests – do not worry about having repeats in the list.

(d) Finally, Mary, who has no faith in Pam's judgement, decides to exclude anyone whom she hates if Pam likes that person. Construct an 'is' query which proves that Harry will not be coming to the party.

(e) Write out the answers to the following query:

```
all(X Y:X likes Harry & Y likes Harry)
```

## Conditionals, new relations and programming

So far, we have only stored facts, in the form of simple sentences, on the database. This does not really constitute a program. One form of program in micro-PROLOG is a database containing facts and new relations composed of conditional sentences. These are also called rules. Rules can be formed from the existing relations using the 'if' keyword. For instance, let us make up a new unary relation called 'disk-type'. An object X is defined to be disk-type if:

```
disks type-is X
```

is a true statement. This effectively finds all the words in the database which are used to describe disks. The word 'if' is needed to describe this new relation, and it can be written directly into the definition. To define this new relation, we use add as before:

```
add(X disk-type if disks type-is X)
```

As with most concepts in micro-PROLOG, to understand this you should read it logically, as you would if it were to appear as a sentence in normal language. The main difference in micro-PROLOG sentences is that they are always rigorously logical, and do not contain the overtones and ambiguities of natural language.

You should be able to search the tree and note that the objects 'floppy' and 'hard' can be described by this new relation 'disk-type' using the above criterion. Thus, the above single addition saves adding the two new sentences:

```
floppy disk-type
hard disk-type
```

However, the database acts as if these two facts were actually present. Thus, if you type in:

```
all(X:X disk-type)
```

the two answers above will be given.

New binary relations can be added in a similar way, and conjunctive sentences can follow the 'if' to form more complex conditions as required. This allows the scope of the database to be extended in any way you wish, by adding in new rules, instead of explicitly adding in all the data items which are implied.

Now try list all, and see how the rule above is stored in the database. It will be stored as a sentence, just as for the facts, but there will be two simple sentences, joined by an 'if'. This finally elevates the database of simple sentences (facts) to the level of a simple program. The storage of rules onto the database, and querying them, is at the basis of micro-PROLOG programming.

To see this new concept further, we will have to construct a more complex database, or the examples chosen will be too simple fully to practise the points raised.

## A micro-PROLOG program

We will have a look at an extension of the rather personal database of the likes and dislikes of Mary and her friends. This supplies an excellent example of a very human situation where logic and inference are somewhat fickle, and a variety of interesting rules govern the behaviour of the relationships which evolve.

Simple micro-PROLOG programming is a question of forming a set of facts and rules on a database. This structure can then be queried, and any complexity of program can be made to result. This is the origin of the expression 'rule-based' programming which is often used for the PROLOG-like languages.

To begin the example, input the following database of facts about four basic relations:

```
Mary likes John
Mary likes Paul
Mary likes George
Mary likes Harry
John likes George
Mary likes Sue
Mary likes Pam
Sue likes Paul
Pam likes George
John male
Paul male
George male
Harry male
Mary female
Sue female
Pam female
Sue frightens Paul
George frightens Harry
Mary frightens Paul
```

This is a set of background facts about these people, and we can deduce many more with a few assumptions, and some extra conditions. For instance, the new relation 'likes-but-frightens' could be added to the database by:

add(X likes-but-frightens Y if X likes Y & X frightens Y)

If you look at the database, you should be able to see which pairs of people satisfy this new relation. Try using the 'all' relation to see if you were right. There are actually two pairs.

Another new relation could be defined by:

```
add(X is-liked-by Y if Y likes X)
```

This definition replaces a total of nine simple facts about which specific people are liked by which others. These would otherwise have to be typed in separately for the new relation. In addition, as the database grows, new 'likes' facts automatically contribute to the 'is-liked-by' relation. Use all, again, to find the pairs satisfying the relation.

We can now ask questions such as:

```
is(Paul liked-by Pam)
```

or

```
all(X:X likes-but-frightens Paul)
```

This allows the original database to be extended in an infinite number of new ways.

A more complex example would be to define a relation called 'can-marry'. Two people are assumed to be able to marry if they are of opposite sex. However, the database above allows us to add in a few more conditions to be able to produce a more accurate result. For instance, it would help if at least one of the potential partners liked the other. This sentence can be translated into:

```
(X can-marry Y if X likes Y & X male & Y female)
```

Which pairs will satisfy this? Work it out before reading on, and then try it, if you can. You may be slightly surprised by the answer.

This certainly does give a possible condition for two people being able to marry. However, it is not the only one. There are other conditions which would involve, for instance, X female and Y male. In other words, we need some way of constructing an 'or' condition so that we can include the first case above, or the second or any other possible combinations which can exist.

You will notice that only the 'and' logical operation has been defined so far, though 'or' is also a SIMPLE word. We will see how to use 'or' in the next chapter, but it is not actually essential because just by storing two conditional sentences for the definition in the database, you are automatically 'oring' them together. The reason is that if the search fails on the first one, it will proceed to look at the next instead. Thus, the two conditions suggested above are implicitly 'ored' together by typing in the following in addition to the last one:

```
(X can-marry Y if X likes Y & X female & Y male)
```

We now have two definitions of 'can-marry' on the database, effectively ored together. Try listing the relation can-marry to see how it is stored. This is a typical program in micro-PROLOG. It consists of a database of facts (simple sentences) and rules. In particular it is a sequence of two definitions, each containing a sequence of three conditions to try out, anded together, so that they all three must be true for the relation to succeed.

We can thus store as many definitions as required to define the 'can-marry' relation. As we proceed with programming in micro-PROLOG you will see that all the normal activities of computer programming can be reproduced using this language, as one would expect. However, the whole presentation is orientated towards natural language and natural logic.

*Example 2.4*

(a) Are there any other definitions involving swops of X and Y which must be added into the 'can-marry' program to ensure that no answers are missed?

(b) Define the 'opposite-sex-to' relation, and use this to define the 'respects' relation defined such that A respects B if B frightens A, and they are of opposite sex.

## Backtracking, evaluation order and variable labels

The process of backtracking, which is one of the most important qualities of the PROLOG languages, is the activity described above whereby the database is searched for one set of solutions to a query, and when those are found, the next in sequence is searched for, and so on. The last example above (Example 2.4 (b)) shows this action quite well, and you should read through the answer at the end of this chapter before reading on. Here, X and Y are looked for such that X is male, and Y is female, then the same male is used, and the next female found. This continues until all females have been included, and the definition backtracks to look for another male before repeating the process.

This backtracking ensures that all possibilities have been covered, and is a very high level or intelligent activity. To set up the same structure in a BASIC-type language would involve a considerable degree of complexity. We will see how important the principle is as we progress through the language.

The above also gives a good example of the method by which micro-PROLOG evaluates queries. The general principles behind this method are the same for all such programs, no matter how complex they become. You should be sure to master the examples above before continuing, as they will be assumed in the following.

The order of evaluation of a query is also important for optimising program execution. For instance, if there were many more males than females in a database, it is worth remembering that a query which contains the phrase:

```
X male & Y female
```

will find one of the few males first, and then wade through every single female, Y, for that X before backtracking to X and sequencing to the next X. This will not matter in many cases, but there are examples where this slows the program down considerably.

Finally, in this subsection, you might have noticed in your own experimentation that micro-PROLOG tends to forget the exact variable labels you have used in your original definition of a relation. For instance, copy the following into your computer, exactly as written below:

```
add(z1 r x2 if z1 male & x2 female)
```

Here, we have defined a general relation which has been called 'r' for convenience, and ease of typing. Now list the 'r' relation, and you will see something like:

```
X r Y  if  X  male  and  Y  female
```

micro-PROLOG has changed the actual labels you have used for the variables z1 and x2 to X and Y. This is because it does not try to remember the labels – just the position of the variables. It will allocate new variable names in a given order starting with X, Y and Z for any variables you may use. It will, of course, religiously preserve the meaning of the definition as it does so.

## Answer generation

Before continuing to the next part of the study of micro-PROLOG, one further concept included in the above must be highlighted. It revolves around the backtracking and seeking for answers to a query described above. It is always necessary to pay attention to the generation of answers to a query. For instance, if you were to write down:

```
all(x y : x male)
```

there would be no way whereby y could be generated from the query condition. Certainly, the x's can, and will, be generated, but the second member of the answer pattern (labelled y here) will remain variable. Thus, the answer to this will be something like:

```
John  X
Paul  X
George  X
Harry  X
```

Note that micro-PROLOG has found all the answers to the first item in the answer pattern, but leaves the second as a variable – which it relabels as X, being the first variable label in its variable name list.

This attention to ensuring that the query condition generates examples of the answer pattern is often forgotten in PROLOG programming, and will be pointed out again later.

This principle does not just hold for queries, it also holds for relation definitions. For instance, if you write:

```
add(X relates-to Y if X female)
```

then no Y's will be generated, and again an 'all' query will provide answers containing variables.

We will see some further examples of the importance of all these principles in the next chapter where arithmetic is considered.

Finally, of the three main logic operations 'and', 'or' and 'not', the first has been defined explicitly, the second can be made implicit within the method of defining relations, and the third, negation, has not yet been defined. Negation has to be used carefully, and we will look at this in the next chapter.

### defined, reserved, dict

It is sometimes useful to find out whether a given alphanumeric constant has already been defined on the database, or whether it is a special micro-PROLOG word, or included on the dict. These questions can be answered using an 'is' query, and one of the three names above. For instance, the word 'male' is not reserved as a special micro-PROLOG word, but it is defined by the example above, and is included on the dict. The following would be used to confirm these facts:

```
is(male reserved)
NO

is(male defined)
YES

is(male dict)
YES
```

If you now kill the definition of male, then all the above queries will give NO for an answer.

### Summary

**Data Types** Only alphanumeric strings containing letters, numbers and hyphens are considered to be alphanumeric constants. Numbers are integer and floating point, and may be used with or without a minus sign, and a decimal point. Plus signs, and bare decimal points with no leading number, are forbidden. Numbers which are too large to be represented as a simple set of digits are automatically represented by E notation.

X, Y and Z, in upper- or lower-case, are the basic variables in micro-PROLOG. More variables may be constructed from these by adding integers as suffixes.

Lists are objects as above separated by spaces, and enclosed in round brackets. A sublist is a list within another list.

**Relations** Relations are basic programming elements of micro-PROLOG. They bind two or more pieces of data together, or describe them. A two-argument relation is called a 'binary' relation, a single argument relation is called a 'unary' relation. Three arguments define a 'ternary' relation. Relations are stored on the current database by typing them in using the 'add' function. micro-PROLOG then uses these relations to answer queries. Further relations can be constructed from if statements, and conjunctions.

**SIMPLE** This is an easily learned and straightforward 'front end processor' which allows a more conversational method of programming in PROLOG. The SIMPLE package has a number of keywords which it uses to produce standard syntax which the micro-PROLOG interpreter can understand. This will become clearer after reading the chapter on the standard syntax of micro-PROLOG.

**add** add is used to add a relation to the database. The relation must follow the add keyword within round brackets.

**accept** This is a keyword which allows a group of facts to be added to the database without using the word add each time.

**list** This keyword can be used to list the whole database, by following it with the word all. Alternatively, the name of a specific relation can follow list, and the items stored against that relation will then be printed out.

**delete** delete can be used to delete a single defined fact on the database, or it can be used to remove a fact in a designated position within the facts stored against a given relation name.

**kill** This word can be used to remove a complete relation on the database, or the whole database itself, to give a clean slate.

**edit** This can be used to call up a given fact or rule on the database, by its position within the database. All aspects of that item can then be altered at will.

**dict** A set called the dictionary is stored on the database, in a normally hidden form. It contains all the words used in the database, and acts as a reference for the data stored there. It is stored in the form of a unary relation, and its contents can be viewed and altered at will.

**load** and **save** These words can be used to store and retrieve the current database. Their use is machine-dependent.

**is** This word, followed by a query within round brackets, commands micro-PROLOG to check on the truth of the statement within the brackets. The answer YES is given if true, and NO if not.

**all, which** and **one** The first two words are identical, either is followed by round brackets containing an answer pattern containing variables, a colon, and a condition which those variables must satisfy. micro-PROLOG then searches through the database, perhaps a number of times, looking for and printing out all values of those variables which do satisfy the conditions given. 'one' is used in the same way, but prints out the answers one at a time.

**Conjunctions** 'and' (or &) is a SIMPLE keyword which may be used to join conditions together logically to give more complex conditions which must be satisfied by the variables in a query. 'or' is another, but is not necessarily needed explicitly, as simply storing several separate rules on the database 'ors' them together. The word 'or' does exist, and is described in the next chapter. 'not' is not a conjunction, but it is one of the three main logical operations and is also described later.

**Backtracking** A set of conditions within a query is executed from left to right, in a 'forward tracking' manner. When this is complete, the interpreter backtracks towards the start of the conditions, executing as it goes, and eventually checks for the next occurrence of an answer for the first condition on the database. Backtracking is responsible for ensuring that all possible answers are found to any given query.

**if** This keyword is used in defining rules. A new rule will be defined 'if' some conditions are satisfied. The conditions have the same form as for relations and query conditions in general, and the new rule is added using 'add'.

**Program** A micro-PROLOG program consists of a database containing a set of facts and rules.

**defined, reserved, dict** These are used to check whether a word defined on the database is a micro-PROLOG reserved word and/or is on the dictionary respectively.

## Solutions to problems

*Example 2.1*

(a) To move 'C before D' to the end of the before relation, note that this item is in the third position, and needs to move to the fifth position. This is done by using:

```
edit before 3
```

and changing the 3 which appears to a 5. In fact, any number greater than 4 will do here, as greater numbers simply result in the member being placed at the end of the list of before members.

To change A before B to B after A, use edit, and retype the whole line using a 2 for the position to ensure that it is stored at the end of the database.

To store the afters onto after1, and the befores onto before1, store the whole database using save onto some intermediate file, such as 'test'. Then kill the befores, and you will be left with the afters, which can then be stored. Now kill all again, load test, kill the afters this time, and thus store the befores onto before1.

Loading after1 followed by before1 simply stores the data in that order in the machine. In general, adding data to the database by any means is performed in order, except that like relations are kept together.

(b) Deleting the first before member is done by:

```
delete before 1
```

The trick is to consider the effect of this action. It removes the first member, and thus the previous second and third members are moved up to first and second place respectively. To delete the old third member, you will have to use:

```
delete before 2
```

instead of 3.

To add the next two members, use:

```
add 1 (H before I)
add 3 (I before J)
```

The first shunts everything down one, and the second puts the next member into third place.

The resulting database is:

```
X after W
B after A
H before I
D before E
I before J
C before D
```

(c) The text contains four statements about painting. The first says that Mary paints an oil of a lamb. This is a relation which binds three objects together. The three objects are Mary, oil and lamb. These can be represented as:

```
paints(Mary oil lamb)
```

Only the prefix notation will do, as there is no other definition of a ternary relation in SIMPLE or in micro-PROLOG in general. The other uses of the paints relation are rather less obvious than the above, but you should be able to sort out the complete database as:

```
paints(Mary oil lamb)
paints(Peter water-colour hills)
paints(famous-artist oil sky)
paints(sky cloud vista)
```

The representation here is not unique. For instance, a whole phrase has been reduced to just the word vista, and oil has been used in the first and third members, despite the use of oils and oil in the text. It is good practice to reduce the number of different representations of the same thing in storing data, because the computer language cannot tell, for instance, that oil and oils are essentially the same word – unless you tell it so. Remember, a certain amount of allowance has to be made for the rather crude nature of the computer. This is also the reason for reducing the words used to the minimum required to make sense of the data.

The only one of these items which should give cause for serious debate is the last one. It is metaphorical – the sky is not a person, and is not able to paint, especially not in clouds. However, the sense of this item should be plain.

This is an important example of the way in which a wide-ranging and typically human text can be reduced to simple relations for later analysis.

*Example 2.2*

(a) YES
(b) NO
(c) micro
(d) no answers at all
(e) micro

Note that even though the answer may contain repeats, the blind sequential search for objects satisfying the conditional sentence simply ploughs through from top to bottom of the database, printing as it goes.

*Example 2.3*

(a) is(George likes X) will give the answer NO.
(b) all(X:Mary likes X)
(c) all(Y:Mary likes X & X likes Y)
(d) is(Mary hates Harry & Pam likes Harry) which gives the answer YES proving the point.
(e) The answers are:

    Pam Pam (because both X and Y can equal Pam)
    Pam Jack
    Jack Pam
    Jack Jack

To understand this list, you should run through the database, looking for X and Y values which satisfy the query condition, including cases where X and Y are equal.

*Example 2.4*

(a) The first condition for 'can-marry' yields no answers for the relation because of the particular facts stored on the database. If it is extended, this first definition may then produce some answers. Either way, the second condition was needed, because when we say that two people can marry if they are of opposite sex and like each other, we mean that either A can like B or B can like A. It is thus necessary to allow for both possibilities. In ensuring that all possibilities are included in the definitions, you should check that X likes Y includes all possible pairs of people who like each other, and then ensure that male and female are checked for X and Y as well as Y and X. This has been achieved by the two definitions given, and no further swops of X and Y will yield any further cases.

(b) The required relation is added to the database by the following:

```
add(X opposite-sex-to Y if X male & Y female)
```

If you look for all X Y pairs which satisfy this relation, you will start by looking for an X which is male. This should be John. A Y which is female is then sought, and Mary is the first on the list of females. Thus X and Y will be John and Mary for the first pair to satisfy this definition. The same male, John, is then used to pair up with the next female (Sue) and so on until no more females remain. The next male is then found and so on. This actually finds all pairs of opposite sex perfectly well. However, it arranges them in male-female order. If this does not matter, then the above definition is sufficient. However, if you ask the question:

```
is( Mary opposite-sex-to George)
```

you would naturally expect the answer to be YES. This is not the case here as female-male pairs are not covered by the definition. The following must be added to complete the relationship 'opposite-sex-to':

```
add(X opposite-sex-to Y if X female & Y male)
```

'respects' is defined as follows:

```
add(X respects Y if Y frightens X
                 & X opposite-sex-to Y)
```

The first sentence following the 'if' certainly generates all the pairs where one is frightened by the other, the second sentence checks each pair to see if they are of opposite sex. This includes all the possible cases, either way round, and thus this definition is complete.

As you can see, order is important in rules, and it is a common mistake to forget this, and thus leave out a whole set of possible facts by the incomplete definition of a relation. Just as in BASIC when you nest FOR loops, it is important to 'dry-run' the definition to ensure that it works in full. Imagine asking 'is' questions as above to ensure that all possible such questions will give the required answer.

# Chapter Three
# Arithmetic and List Processing

## Introduction

The last chapter introduced some of the basics of micro-PROLOG programming. It gave examples of the main keywords which the SIMPLE 'front-end' supplies, and introduced program evaluation and backtracking. We will look at programming techniques in more detail in the next chapter. This chapter provides a few more basic keywords, shows you how to do arithmetic, and how lists are defined in micro-PROLOG. These two areas provide examples of the ideas presented in the previous chapter, and introduce more of the 'nuts and bolts' before proceeding to the more complex concepts of micro-PROLOG programming.

micro-PROLOG is not really a language for general numeric application, or for scientific work, and if large numeric calculations are required, BASIC is probably better suited. This chapter uses your familiarity with programming to build further in describing a more rule-based and logical programming procedure.

We will use the in-built arithmetic and logical facilities of micro-PROLOG and SIMPLE rather than the more general mathematical notation which you can use if you load in one of the extra modules which usually comes with the main language. If you wish to write serious numeric and scientific programs, once you have mastered the language, you can refer to your manual, and use the appropriate module to take this chapter further.

Finally, we will look at two more logical operations – namely 'or' and negation. The 'or' operation can be performed by storing several rules on the database, but it is often neater to use the word 'or' instead. Also, the last chapter defined all of its relations in terms of positive statements. In general, it is important to be able to use 'not' as well as 'and' and 'or'. Both 'or' and 'not' must be used carefully in micro-PROLOG, and once you have assimilated the data in this chapter, you will be able to understand these new operations as a precursor to the more complex programming techniques of the rest of the book.

### Numeric operations

As mentioned in a previous chapter, there are several ways to write the arithmetic operations of addition, subtraction, multiplication and division. PROLOG probably adopts one of the most eccentric, but intelligent in computing. There is no subtraction function, only addition, and there is no division function, only multiplication. The two operations left out are generated from the others. In addition, there are more arithmetic functions for the comparison operations such as less-than, and for checking integer answers. We will look at these in the following sections.

### Addition and subtraction

The keyword SUM, in upper-case, is used for both addition and subtraction. The definition is as follows:

```
SUM(X Y Z)   is equivalent to   X + Y = Z
```

It can be regarded, among other things, as a true statement concerning three numbers. You can ask the question:

```
is(SUM(7 4 11))
```

and expect the answer YES. In addition:

```
SUM(X 4 11)
```

will be true if X has been passed the value 7 by a previous relation or function.

micro-PROLOG also attempts to make the statement true if one of its arguments is left unknown. This is the origin of its use to solve problems and generate new numbers, as we shall see.

SUM is used, for instance, in the following manner:

```
all(Z:SUM(3 4 Z))
```

which has the solution:

    7

Thus, the SUM function is queried just as for any other operation in micro-PROLOG. The first two numbers are added together and stored in the variable written in the third place.

The above use of the SUM function is to generate a number satisfying the relationship:

$$3 + 4 = Z$$

This generating facility is an important one for functions, and the number generated can be used by subsequent relations and functions in a definition such as:

```
(TRIPLUS(X1 X2 X3 Z) if SUM(X1 X2 Y) & SUM(Y X3 Z))
```

This is a definition of a new function, TRIPLUS, which works on three numbers, and stores their sum in the fourth variable in the TRIPLUS function. When TRIPLUS is used, three numbers are plugged into the first three places, and the last is left as a variable. For instance in

```
all(X:TRIPLUS(3 4 5 X))
```

the answer will be 12. The process of dealing with this evaluation begins by plugging 3 and 4 into the first SUM in the TRIPLUS definition. This generates the value of Y as 7 which is then passed onto the second SUM, along with the value of X3, and this generates the value of Z, which is passed back to the variable in the fourth place of the TRIPLUS function, whatever it may be called. Remember, the position of variables is more important than their actual names. Notice how the process proceeds from left to right. If it did not, the second SUM would be unsolvable – it has too many variables until the first SUM is executed.

Another aspect of SUM, as mentioned above, is its ability to be queried for the truth of a statement. For instance, if you were not sure that 34 plus 68 was 102, you could use the following:

```
is(SUM(34 68 102))
```

and receive the answer YES. This also holds for composite micro-PROLOG functions and relations. For instance, if you were not sure that 3 plus 4 plus 5 equalled 12, the following could be used to reassure you:

```
is(TRIPLUS(3 4 5 12))
YES
```

Here, SUM and TRIPLUS are not being used as generating functions, but rather as relations between their arguments.

To take the generating facility of SUM further, consider how one subtracts numbers in general. 4 can be subtracted from 7 by looking for a number which when added to 4 would give 7. The micro-PROLOG method of setting this up is as follows:

```
all(X:SUM(X 4 7))
```

The answer will be given as 3. SUM is being used here to generate a number which when placed in its first argument will make the SUM expression true. This is the basic method behind all of micro-PROLOG's evaluation of arithmetic, and other, functions. If you can pick up the habit of thinking in this manner, you will find programming in micro-PROLOG, and all other dialects of the language, straightforward.

Now try the following:

```
all(X:SUM(4 X 7))
```

This is the same as above, but with the first two arguments transposed.

Again the answer is 3, as you would expect from the logic of the function. Again, micro-PROLOG is looking for a number which when added to 4 gives 7. Whether you add this number to 4, or add 4 to it, the answer is the same. If, on the other hand you commute the 7 and the 4 to give

```
all(X:SUM(7 X 4))
```

then the logic is used to find a number which when added to 7 gives 4. This gives −3, just as in the normal form:

```
7 + (- 3) = 4
```

We can generate numbers which lie in any of the three arguments of SUM. However, there is a restriction to this generation process. The rule is that there must be a unique answer for the number to be generated. If you try

```
all(X Y : SUM(X Y 6))
```

for instance, an error will result. There is an infinite number of answers to this query. The rule to remember in micro-PROLOG is simply that you should never try to ask questions to which you know there are too many answers to be practical – reasonable enough if you think about it!

SUM may also be used as part of the definition of a relation to impose query conditions. For instance:

```
(X zeros Y if SUM(X Y 0))
```

This defines the 'zeros' relation which is true if one of the arguments can zero the other by addition. This also implies that X and Y are equal but of different sign, unless they are both zero.

As with micro-PROLOG relations in general, it can be used to generate answers in order to make itself true, as well as being used to check on the truth of a statement. For instance,

```
all(X : X zeros 5)
```

will give the answer −5 as expected. This can be used to generate the negative of a given number to be passed onto another relation or function. For instance, the definition of a subtraction function could be:

```
subtract(X Y Z)  equivalent to  X - Y = Z
```

and this would give a negative answer for Z if Y is greater than X. A rather long-winded definition would be:

```
(subtract(X Y Z) if X1 zeros Y & SUM(X X1 Z))
```

This method of evaluation of subtract starts by using zeros to generate a value for X1 which is the negative of the value of subtract's second argument. The next step would be to pass this on to the SUM in the last part of the definition of subtract. The SUM then generates the required answer in Z, and passes this back to the last argument of subtract. You should think of the definition above in this sequential left-to-right manner, just as you would for a program in BASIC where statements on the same line are separated by colons.

Theoretically, we can now use the nature of the language to query the subtract function to generate numbers for its arguments, or to check on the truth of a subtract statement. An example of the latter would be:

```
is(subtract(13 3 10))
```

The answer is YES. There is no problem with this use of subtract because all the numbers are given, and these are simply plugged into the definition, calculated accordingly – and either all the numbers in the arguments tie up, in which case the answer is true, or YES, or they do not in which case NO is given.

The situation is more complex, however, when new numbers are to be generated by the subtract function. You can run into problems using definitions backwards, unless they have been constructed to be fully reversible. For instance, the following example does work:

```
all(X:subtract(X 4 -1))
```

and the program gives the answer as 3. It is worth following the process for this case, so that the next example will be understandable. When the above is typed in, micro-PROLOG looks at the definition of subtract, substitutes 4 and −1 for the second and third arguments, and then looks at the next part of the definition. The zeros function which follows takes the second argument, 4, and uses it to set X1 to −4. This is then transferred to the last part of the definition, where the SUM is given two arguments, and produces the third which it passes back to the first argument of subtract. This is then the value of X which is printed. At no time is any function in the definition asked to generate an answer from too little data – each part of the definition has all but one value given to it, and only has to generate the single value as an answer.

Now consider the following:

```
all(X:subtract(3 X -1))
```

When the zeros is evaluated, it still has two variables, because the second argument of subtract above, is passed on to it at the start of the evaluation. The program fails at that point. You will see an error which tells you that there are too many variables in the SUM within the definition of zeros. Thus, even though you should be able to generate new values simply by leaving a variable in one of the arguments, this is only possible if the definition is written to be fully reversible. It is not possible simply to add a further definition to the database to take account of this case as the evaluation will founder on the first definition, cease execution and give an error.

To sum up, the definition of SUM can be used to generate numbers in any of its arguments, as well as allowing the truth of a numeric statement to be checked. Functions and relations defined from existing ones, however, will not allow generation of new numbers unless they are defined to be fully reversible.

## Multiplication and division

Just as subtraction can be considered as the reverse of addition, so division is the reverse of multiplication. Again, there is only one (upper-case) keyword TIMES for multiplication, and division comes from it by using the function in reverse.

TIMES is defined as follows:

```
TIMES(X Y Z)   equivalent to  X * Y = Z
```

Thus,

```
all(Z:TIMES(3 4 Z))
```

has the answer 12. Similarly,

```
all(Z:TIMES(16 Z 4))
```

has the answer 0.25, and,

```
all(Z:TIMES(Z 16 4))
```

has the answer 0.25.

Incidentally, remember to put a 0 in front of a fractional decimal number. If you write .25 instead of 0.25 you will cause an error or an incorrect answer.

Division is simply a matter of using TIMES to generate a number which when multiplied by a second gives the number in the third argument place. micro-PROLOG will backtrack to find the answer whichever place it is in. An error will be caused by asking TIMES to divide a number by zero. Thus, for instance, TIMES(0 X 4) is not allowed.

As with SUM, this function can be used at will to generate numbers for transfer to the next stage in a rule. For instance, division could be written as:

```
div(X Y Z)  equivalent to  X/Y = Z
```

(with Y non-zero) and defined by:

```
(div(X Y Z) if TIMES(Y Z X))
```

This uses the fact that dividing X by Y to give Z is the same as saying find numbers such that Y multiplied by Z is X. You should write this down to ensure that you agree before continuing. The definition of div is completely reversible, because it simply transfers its three arguments straight to TIMES which is itself fully reversible. Again, the main rule to remember is not to use more than one unknown in its arguments. The other rule is not to divide by zero.

## Number types

As with BASIC, the numbers in micro-PROLOG can be integers, floating point or exponential format. Thus, 50000 can be represented as 5E4. In fact if a calculation causes the answer to be too long to fit into a single number, the number will automatically be represented in exponential format.

Your manual will tell you how accurately your version of the language stores numbers. You can generally assume that at least 8 digits of accuracy are kept, that integers range from −32767 to 32767, and that exponents range from −127 to 127. No number in micro-PROLOG should start with anything but a digit or a minus sign. + signs are not allowed before numbers, numbers are assumed positive unless preceded by a minus sign. Exponents may only be integers, and again may only be preceded by a minus sign, never a plus. Remember that in any conjunctive definition involving several arithmetic functions, as in TRIPLUS or subtract defined above, the order of execution is strictly logical, from left to right. Thus, unlike in BASIC, an addition may be executed before a multiplication, or vice versa depending upon which is placed first in the definition or query condition.

We can now look at some numeric examples to practise the functions and principles described above.

*Example 3.1*

(a) Define the 'tri-mult' function which multiplies three numbers together. Is it fully reversible?

(b) Define backdiv(X Y Z) such that Y/X=Z. Is it fully reversible?

(c) Define the 'inverse-of' function such that X inverse-of Y if X is one over Y. Is it fully reversible?

(d) How would you try to define the SQRT-OF function, to find the square root, in terms of a single TIMES function, and would it work? If not, explain why not.

## LESS and EQ

There are two keywords supplied for comparison in arithmetic work, LESS and EQ. All others come from them. These are binary relations, and may be used in the prefix or infix forms.

LESS is used to check whether one number is smaller than another. It cannot be used alone to generate a number less than another, as such a number would not be unique. There is an infinite number of numbers less than a given number.

LESS can be used in a query, or a query condition. For instance, (using the prefix form),

```
is(LESS(3 6))
```

has the answer YES, and the following:

```
add(LESSEQ(X Y) if LESS(X Y))
add(LESSEQ(X Y) if TIMES(-1 Y Z) & SUM(X Z O))
```

is a way of adding a rather clumsy definition of a less than or equal relation called LESSEQ. This definition has two parts stored on the database. The first will give LESSEQ a true answer if LESS is true, and the second multiplies one of the arguments of LESSEQ by −1, and adds this to the other to see if zero results. If it does, then X and Y must be equal. This is another example of 'oring' conditions by storing separate rules on the database.

A better definition of LESSEQ would come from using the EQ relation which is also available. This relation can be used both in queries and as a number generator. Thus, using EQ in the infix form,

```
is(4 EQ 4)
```

would have the answer YES, and the following

```
all(X:X EQ 4)
```

would generate the number 4 for X. A better definition for LESSEQ would be:

```
(X LESSEQ Y if X LESS Y)
(X LESSEQ Y if X EQ Y)
```

Notice that this uses the infix form throughout, though prefix would do just as well, as for all binary functions and relations. If a LESSEQ query is used, the first of the above sentences is checked, and the answer given is YES if true. If not, the usual micro-PROLOG search causes the next sentence to be used, and again YES is the answer if true. If still not true, the database continues to be searched for facts about LESSEQ, but finds no more and eventually gives the answer NO.

*Example 3.2*

(a) In BASIC you should be familiar with five comparison relations between numbers. Three of them have been introduced above. Define the other two in micro-PROLOG.

(b) In the above, it was stated that LESS cannot generate numbers, but EQ can. Using the second definition of LESSEQ, i.e. the one using EQ, will this generate any numbers in a query such as the following?

```
all(X:X LESSEQ 4)
```

If not, how can it be changed slightly to give an answer to this before causing an error?

(c) Can you think of a way to shorten the second rule in the definition of LESSEQ even further?

## INT

Another important numeric relation is INT which will both check that a number is integral, and will generate the integer part of a floating point number. It has a unary and a binary form. As usual, the binary form can use infix or prefix notation.

In the unary form, INT is used to check that a given number is integral. Thus, the following can be written:

```
is(3 INT)
```

and the answer will be YES. This cannot be used to generate integers – there are simply too many of them! If a variable is used for the argument above, it must have a value before this is reached.

The binary form of INT is used to generate the integer part of a number. Thus, the following:

```
all(X:4.56 INT X)
```

has the answer 4, and the following:

```
all(X: -4.56 INT X)
```

has the answer −5. Note that INT always rounds down. Also, observe that a space is needed, in general, after the colon if it is followed by a minus sign as in the second example. You can check this type of detail for yourself in your particular version of the language.

In apparent contradiction to previous cases, INT, in the binary form, cannot be used to check that a given number is the integer part of another number. The rules of use of INT demand that the second argument is always an unknown. To check that a given integer is the integer part of another number, its integer part must be found, and then compared with the given integer using EQ. Thus, the following checks that 5 is the integer part of 5.43:

```
is(5.43 INT X & X EQ 5)
```

and this has the answer YES. Here, the use of INT produces a value for X which is then passed as usual to the next relation, EQ in this case.

## A programming example

Numeric calculations are easy to set up and solve, and can thus be used to practise the basic principles of programming in micro-PROLOG, even if you do not intend to produce arithmetic routines later.

Using the basic keywords above, we can perform all the usual mathematical functions – For instance, the calculation of divisional remainders, which are used in a number of ways in computing. We will now use the INT function to find the remainder, and the integer part of the result of division.

The most important initial decisions to make in micro-PROLOG programming are to think of a name for the function, how many arguments it will have, and how they will be defined. Remainder is a ternary relation, as it takes two numbers, divides them, finds the result and calculates the remainder which it passes to the third argument. Thus, we will be defining the function

```
rem(X Y Z)
```

which calculates X/Y, finds the integer part, subtracts it from X/Y, multiplies by Y, and passes the result to Z. You should study this if your arithmetic is a little rusty, or refer to a maths book for the definition and meaning of remainder. As usual, these actions will have to be confined to one or more database rules containing 'if', and may be written as follows:

```
(rem(X Y Z) if . . . . . . . )
```

The dots above will be replaced by a set of simple sentences which pass variable values from left to right, as in previous examples. The first operation is division:

```
(rem(X Y Z) if TIMES(X1 Y X) . . . )
```

This assumes that X and Y are given, and asks for a value of X1 which when multiplied by Y gives X. This is the same as dividing X by Y to give X1. This value can then be passed on to any further calculations. The next step is to find the integer part of this division, as it may have a fractional part:

```
(rem(X Y Z) if TIMES(X1 Y X) & X1 INT X2 . . .)
```

This has so far produced two values. One is X1, the floating point division of X and Y, and the other is X2, the integer part of this division. The difference between the two multiplied by Y is the remainder. Thus the final operation subtracts X2 from X1 and multiplies by Y. This gives:

```
(rem(X Y Z) if TIMES(X1 Y X) & X1 INT X2
                & SUM(X2 X3 X1) & TIMES(X3 Y Z))
```

This is the final definition, and as with all arithmetic calculations, the order of the processes within the program is crucial. The program goes wrong if X and Y are not both given, or if one of them is negative. The latter is due to the fact that INT does not round off towards zero for negative numbers.

## A programming method

The above gives an excellent example of micro-PROLOG programming, and the main points can be summarised as follows:

(1) Start by naming the relation which will be needed.
(2) Define the arguments of the relation.
(3) Consider the logic of the various operations needed, and construct a routine.
(4) Pay careful attention to those arguments which must be given values for the program to succeed.

There are some parallels with BASIC in this method, mainly in terms of the sequence of operations required to attain the end.

This completes the basics of numeric calculations in micro-PROLOG. Some of the above is useful in general micro-PROLOG programming, particularly if you wish to write statistical or probability routines. In addition, arithmetic examples show up some of the fundamental processes of the language such as backtracking and methods of evaluation.

*Example 3.3*
(a) Write a program for the ternary 'between' relation to define when a number is between two others, but not equal to either. Extend this to the 'within-range' relation which is the same, but allows the number to equal one of the bounds. Can these relations be used to generate numbers, or are they purely for checking?

(b) Write a program for a function to check that the cube of a given number is less than 1000.

## Artificial intelligence

Much of artificial intelligence is concerned with the comprehension of sentences in natural language. micro-PROLOG is well adapted to converting such sentences into a form which is very human in its use of rules and pattern matching. For instance, we are often confronted with questions such as: 'How many apples can I get for 75 pence if they are 17 pence each, and how much, if anything, will be left over after buying them?

It is not usual for us to consider the intricacies of long division or numeric approximation when solving this sort of problem in a busy greengrocer's queue! Most people will solve this type of problem by using a form of subtraction or addition, and a type of pattern matching. We are trying to match the number of apples with 75 pence, given that 17 pence is matched with a single apple. The routine is probably something like: '2 apples are 34 pence, one more makes 51 pence, that leaves 24 pence, which will buy the fourth apple leaving 7 pence over'

There are endless variations on this theme, of course, and often such calculations will be consciously or unconsciously attended with counting actions using the fingers – further pattern matching to do with numeric mnemonics, which were at the basis of the abacus and other early calculating machines.

The above calculation is child's play to code into any computer language, but the approach will differ between BASIC-type languages and PROLOG-type languages. In BASIC, the calculation would probably be done using mathematical formulae which would have to be constructed using a fair amount of conceptual mathematics:

```
X = INT(75/17)
Y = (75/17 - X)*17
PRINT "No. Apples = ";X
PRINT "Amount left over = ";Y
```

This requires a mental understanding of the mathematical format for the abstract calculation which must be performed to find the number of apples, and the remainder.

It is true that micro-PROLOG will still use some abstract mathematics of a sort, particularly for finding the remainder. However, it is easy to construct a human version of the micro-PROLOG program.

We know that there is a whole number of apples which when multiplied by 17 pence is the number of apples you can 'fit' into 75 pence. This is a clear pattern-matching routine which uses the TIMES function followed by INT to remove the fractional part, if any:

```
which(X:TIMES(X1 17 75) & X1 INT X)
```

This works out the number of apples which will fit into 75 pence, including a fraction of an apple, and then removes the fraction of an apple to give the first part of the answer. As indicated above, the next step would be to find out how much has been spent on the X apples in the calculation, and then subtract that from 75 pence. This part of the routine can be added in as follows:

```
which(No. apples = X  Amount left over = Y:TIMES(X1 17 75)
              & X1 INT X & TIMES(X 17 X2) & SUM(Y X2 75))
```

Note the direct use of comments to make the output more acceptable and readable.

*Example 3.4*

This last example contains a simple routine which proceeds from left to right, passes values forward in the routine, and finally fills in the required variable values. One problem with this query is that it is not stored on the database. As with a BASIC routine which has no line-numbers, it is lost once it has executed. How would you store the routine on the database for future use, and how would you use it?

## Lists

To extend the idea of writing programs which mirror human language we need to look at list processing. This is a powerful method of considering sets of objects rather than single alphanumeric constants. A natural language sentence may be regarded as a list, and processing this for the individual members is the first step towards understanding the sentence.

To achieve the best from a study of micro-PROLOG, you should begin to examine the way in which you use natural language. Imagine how you would translate some of the logic of the sentences you use naturally, into a micro-PROLOG form. The study of lists will help considerably in this analysis.

As mentioned before, a list is a set of objects surrounded by round brackets. It is a method of associating objects together for some purpose. For instance, all the people whom Mary likes in the 'likes' database example could be written as:

```
(John Paul George Harry Sue Pam)
```

This is a list of six objects. If we section male and female members out, and write them in separate lists, we have:

```
(John Paul George Harry)  and  (Sue Pam)
```

The first list has four members, and the second has two. We can even combine them together as:

```
((John Paul George Harry) (Sue Pam))
```

Note that there are round brackets around the whole list to contain its members as usual. This list has two members, each of which happens to be a list. We often refer to lists contained within other lists as 'sublists'.

In micro-PROLOG, lists are treated on a similar level to an alphanumeric constant, or a number. This means that just as a variable can have a numeric or an alphanumeric value, it can also have a list value. For instance, we can store Mary's 'likes' in the following way:

```
(Mary likes (John Paul George Harry))
```

This contains the same information as the first four members of the 'likes' database for Mary, but is treated as a completely new piece of information. You can query for it just as for the others if you wish:

```
all(X:Mary likes X)
```

This will give an answer such as:

```
John
Paul
George
Harry
Sue
Pam
(John Paul George Harry)
```

As you can see, the list is treated as a new object, and the interpreter cannot be expected to understand the relationship between the list members and the others unless you tell it.

The list of objects can be regarded as a neat and compact form of a set of simple sentences. The single list fact added above could be regarded as replacing the first four simple sentences stored on the database. However, the problem is to release that data in a usable form. To this end, we look shortly at how to take a list apart. Before that, however, we will look at how to use some simple lists by extending the last example.

## Using lists

We will rewrite some of the 'likes' database in terms of lists, and then see some of the aspects of using queries on lists, and how useful they can be.

You should clear the current database and load in the following set of facts:

```
(Mary likes (John Paul George Harry))
(Mary likes (Sue Pam)
(John likes (George Paul Harry))
(John likes (Mary Pam Sue))
(George likes (Paul Harry John))
(Pam likes (George Paul Harry))
(Pam likes (Sue Mary))
(Sue likes (Mary))
Mary female
Sue female
Pam female
John male
Paul male
George male
Harry male
```

Note that the last 'likes' sentence shows that Sue only likes one person, and to keep the database consistent, that person, Mary, has been placed within brackets to form a list – with only one member. You must not confuse lists with their members. For instance, if you now try:

```
is(Sue likes Mary)
```

you will see that the answer is NO despite the fact that the opposite appears to be true. The interpreter takes you seriously about the exact form of the objects you are calling up. Mary and (Mary) are completely different objects, and only by telling the computer that they are the same will it make that connection. If you were to add the fact:

```
(Sue likes Mary)
```

the answer to the last query would be YES.

There are two special types of list in list processing. One type is the 'singleton' type of list, which simply means a list containing a single member. You will see why this is important as we progress through the language. The other important list is the empty list. In many ways, paradoxically, this is the most important list in list processing. It is written as () – i.e. two round brackets with nothing between them. Again, you will see why this is so important shortly.

We can write queries in the usual way, except that in the pattern matching used to answer the queries, we can use the form of the lists in the database to sort out the answers. For instance, in the old 'likes' database, we would have had trouble asking questions such as 'how many people like exactly 3 other people'. You should be able to see that the answer to this question is John, George and Pam. The query to write down is:

```
all(X:X likes (X1 X2 X3))
```

This will give John's name twice as micro-PROLOG does not cut out repeats – it might miss something if it did. As you can see, we have simply chosen a list pattern in the query which is a general three-member list. micro-PROLOG will now scan the database matching X up with each object which likes someone, and then check whether the object being liked matches the general three-member list given.

If we ask

```
all(X:X likes (X1))
```

The only answer will be Sue. To ask more complex questions is simply a matter of forming the right query pattern. For instance, suppose we are interested in all the three member lists of people who are male, and liked by John. This translates to:

```
all(X:John likes X & X EQ (X1 X2 X3) & X1 male
                     & X2 male & X3 male))
```

Here, EQ, which works for lists as well as numbers, has been used as a query condition. It ensures that only patterns looking like three-member lists are found for X. The constituents of X are then passed forward for checking by the male conditions.

This example should give you a clue as to how to take lists apart, and find the individual members. The solution is to use a pattern for each member.

## List processing

To take lists apart, we need to start at the beginning, and move sequentially through the list. We read from left to right in western languages, and thus list processing is usually performed in that direction. The order of the members within the list is fixed, and thus the extreme left-hand member of a list holds a special place, being the first member in some sense. This first member, in fact, has a special name – it is called the 'head' of the list.

Humans like to think of routines sequentially, a small bit at a time, and it is useful, therefore, to imagine processing a list from the head forwards. In this context, it is normal to think of a list as having a head and a tail. The head is the first member, and the tail is the rest of the list. Of course, either of these objects may actually be empty. For instance, the head of the empty list is empty. The tail of any singleton list is also empty. However, apart from extreme examples such as this, most lists have a single member, which may be a sublist as a head, and a list as a tail. For instance:

```
(A B C D)   has head A and tail (B C D)

(A B (C D)) has head A and tail (B (C D))

((This is a sublist) this is the tail)
 has
(This is a sublist)     as its head, and
(this is the tail)      as its tail
```

To find the head and tail of a list, a list of variables is matched to it, and the head variable will be matched equal to the head of the given list.

For instance, let us try to find the head of the list of four people whom Mary likes. Look at the database, and see if you can isolate this person. When you have, try the following:

```
all(X:Mary likes (X X1 X2 X3))
```

This will cause the 'likes' part of the database to be searched for all the four member lists matching the pattern given here. When one is found, the head of the list is matched with X, and printed as a solution. The next step is to backtrack to the database again, and find the next four-member list. This provides no further solutions, as you should be able to see by looking at the database.

By this means, we can extract any member of a list, as long as we know how long it is. We will see later how to find the head of a general list.

The tail is found in a similar way. For instance;

```
all((X2 X3 X4):Mary likes (X1 X2 X3 X4))
```

Again, the method of finding an object, the tail of a list in this case, is to construct a general pattern for it, and then construct a query condition to find it.

*Example 3.5*

(a) Write down the tail of each three-member list of people whom John likes, and then construct a query to print these out.

(b) Write down the head of the head of:

(i) ((A B C) D E)
(ii) (((A B) C D) E F)
(iii)(A B C D)

(c) Write down the tail of the tail of the tail of:

(i) (A B C D E)
(ii) (A B C)
(iii)(A (B C D) (E F) ((A) B))

This takes care of processing the members of a list of known fixed length, but we still cannot find the head or tail of a list of unknown length. The trouble is, we have no pattern to match with a general list.

## Lists of unknown length

micro-PROLOG has another symbol which will help define a general list pattern. It is the 'followed by' symbol, and is written as a vertical stroke. Some keyboards and computer screens may not have this symbol, or may print it up as a vertically elongated colon. Your manual should tell you how to type this symbol if it is a problem.

Its use is in sectioning a list into two parts – the first part is followed by the second. For instance, the head of any list is followed by its tail. We can write this, for one of the examples above, as:

```
the list (A B C D)  equals   (A | B C D)
```

which may seem obvious, or of no particular use, but this simple expedient provides a method of writing a general pattern for any list. It comes from the statement in the second sentence of this paragraph, and can be restated as:

'any list is made up of a head followed by a tail'

This allows us to write any list as:

```
(X | Y)
```

The important mental leap to make is to consider Y as a list, namely the tail of this general list, and X as the head, which may be a list or a single member as we have seen. Given this pattern in a query condition, micro-PROLOG will match the head of any given non-empty list with X, and the tail with Y, regardless of length.

For instance, to find the head of every list of people in our database, we could ask for:

```
all(X1:Y likes (X1 | X2))
```

This will search the database for a 'likes' relation, and having found one will match up Y and (X1 | X2) with the person liking, and the list which is liked respectively. Once this match has been made, X1 will be matched to the head, and X2 to the tail. X1 is then printed. micro-PROLOG then backtracks to the database again and continues its search, repeating this procedure for every 'likes' relation it finds. Try it! You should then view the database for yourself, and check that you agree. The intelligent way that you check these answers will be very similar to the artificially intelligent way micro-PROLOG does it.

We can now ask quite complex questions of a database, and it is no longer necessary to know the form of any lists which may be needed. However, we can force a certain type of pattern on the lists concerned if we wish. For instance, we might want to find all of those people who like more than two people. In this case we are searching for people who like lists of people with three or more members. Again, just check the database and satisfy yourself that you know which people are concerned. To ask this sort of question we need a list pattern which ensures at least three members. The following is such a pattern:

```
(X1 X2 X3 | X4)
```

which is a list with three members followed by a tail of any number of members from zero upwards. The pattern written before the '|' symbol is taken to be a set of members at the head of the list matching this pattern. The object written after the symbol can also be given a list pattern, but will simply be matched up with the rest of the list, and is always a list, even if empty.

To use the pattern above, we construct the following query:

```
all(X:X likes (X1 X2 X3 | X4))
```

By now you should be able to tell how micro-PROLOG tackles this query. The database is searched for an X which likes something. That something is then matched up to the pattern shown. If it only has two or one members, there will be no match for X3 – the third member above – and the test fails. Backtracking returns micro-PROLOG to the search, and so on. When a three member list is found, for instance, X1, X2 and X3 match with members successfully, and X4 matches with the empty list. This is perfectly allowable, but the first three individual members may not be matched with the empty member – there is no such object in micro-PROLOG. If there were such an object, this type of pattern matching for lists of a certain length would fail.

We now have a general method of defining lists of any type, and defining queries of almost any complexity. This completes the main part of the 'nuts and bolts' of micro-PROLOG in terms of special symbols and keywords. As you can see, there is a considerably smaller set of such standard devices than may be found in even the most rudimentary version of BASIC, or similar languages. However, you will find that the complexity of micro-PROLOG is more a matter of the use of the above facilities and discovering new programming concepts than learning many more special words. There are still one or two more words to learn, and they will be introduced as they are needed.

After some more examples, the last part of this chapter introduces 'or' and negation, and then we proceed to one of the most important programming concepts available in a serious AI language – namely recursion. As a foretaste of this crucial procedure, note that many of the concepts of other programming languages have their analogies with the work so far in micro-PROLOG, but there is one which so far is missing. We have not yet looked at a specific procedure for looping. It is true that the method of sequentially searching a database could be argued to be analogous to following a loop to its conclusion, and indeed there is a certain amount of repetition in this process. However, the idea of repeating a process, and perhaps keeping a count in some way has not been introduced. Recursion puts this right in the next chapter.

*Example 3.6*

(a) Construct a program for printing out all the third members of the lists of people who are liked by someone. The clue is to find a pattern which contains the third member, and query for this.

(b) Construct a program to print out the list of people liked by the head of the list of males liked by Mary, and then by George.

(c) Construct a program to form a list of the tails of lists of females liked by Mary and John. Can you explain the special list form which this program produces?

(d) Construct a program to print out the tail of the tail of the list (A (B C D) E F).

## (either...or...)

This has been left until now for two reasons. Firstly it is important to realise that storing several rules on a database for a given relation effectively 'ors' them together. In fact, this often gives a clearer definition of the rule than the use of 'or'. Secondly, the use of 'or' is a little involved, and may have clouded the main issues if it had been introduced earlier. However, you will see how important this construction is later, where decision branches in a complex program have to be translated into 'ored' sentences.

The use of 'or' is to bind together several rules into a single statement. For instance, if we wish to define the meaning of 'person' in the above database, we might use the fact that a person is either male or female. Thus, we could define person as:

```
(X person if X male)
(X person if X female)
```

These rules give a complete definition of person.

To use 'or', the form of the operation is:

(either...or...)

The word 'either' and the brackets are used to ensure that micro-PROLOG knows which two statements to 'or' together. For instance, the following defines person:

```
(X person if (either X male or X female))
```

The relation within the brackets following the 'if' is the complete relation to which that if refers. It may be composed of several other relations joined using & and 'or' in this form, to produce a compound relation.

An example of a nested 'or' would be to find which people liked one, two or three people. This is different from previous examples where we looked for lists of two or more people, for instance. To solve this problem, we have to define the conditions separately. For instance, the following would work:

```
all(X:X likes (X1))
all(X:X likes (X1 X2))
all(X:X likes (X1 X2 X3))
```

This is straightforward, but may be compacted into a single query:

```
all(X:(either X likes (X1) or
      (either X likes (X1 X2) or
              X likes (X1 X2 X3))))
```

As you can see, nesting is performed just as for BASIC numeric calculations, by using brackets to move down into the nested levels. If you stare at this for long enough you will find that you can logically decipher it. However, in many ways the three separate queries are simpler to read and easier to construct.

The relation used in an 'or' condition can be a conjunctive construction, using &. Thus, to find every female who likes two people, and every male who likes three people, we could write:

```
X likes (X1 X2) & X female
```

or

```
X likes (X1 X2 X3) & X male
```

These two 'anded' conditions fit into a single 'or' as follows:

```
all(X:(either X likes (X1 X2) & X female
           or X likes (X1 X2 X3) & X male))
```

The brackets bind together the conditions before and after the 'or', and ensures that micro-PROLOG does not become confused.

One of the main advantages of the use of 'or' is in queries such as:

```
all(X:(either Mary likes X or John likes X))
```

This is neat and easy to read, and saves writing the two queries for X out in full.

## Negation

So far, all statements in query conditions have been positive. For instance, find all the people whom Mary likes, or all the people who are male. It is also possible, as with any other language, to pose the negative of a condition. The SIMPLE keyword, familiarly enough, is 'not' (lower-case), and it needs a certain amount of care in use. It cannot be used to generate answers, only to check them. To find all the females on the database, it is tempting, for instance, to ask something like:

```
all(X:not X male)
```

This will not work as X is not defined before being used within the negated condition. Thus, even though 'male' can be used to generate answers, 'not ... male' cannot.

For the above query condition to be used, we must place a 'generating' condition before it to ensure that X is passed onto the negated condition with a value. This can then be checked and discarded if not applicable, or accepted as a solution as the case may be. A possible generating function might be 'X person' as defined above.

The following would be a way of using the negated condition:

```
all(X:X person & not X male)
```

This is rather a simple example, but it makes the point that 'not' cannot be used to generate objects within the database. It can only be used to check on members passed to it.

It is typical of many routines in micro-PROLOG that a generating condition be required by a subsequent relation. It is an extension of the idea introduced in the arithmetic sections above where a numeric function often required a previous calculation to pass on values and make the later function valid.

Negation is also common in defining other numeric relations from the LESS relation. For instance, greater than or equal, GRTREQ, can be written as:

```
(X GRTREQ Y if not Y LESS X)
```

This relation is only ever used to check on the relation between two given numbers, and as such X and Y above will always be defined. This is necessary to ensure that the negation works.

A more complex example would be to define the 'unsociable' relation such that someone is said to be unsociable, according to the existing database, if they do not specifically like two or more people.

As you should know by now, the skill of micro-PROLOG programming comes in being able to apply logic to a statement such as the one above, and translate it into a program which will include all the possibilities and no more. In examining the statement, it is of help at the start to consider some examples. For instance, if you look at the database, Sue likes just one person, and should be included in the 'unsociable' class as she clearly does not like two or more people. The definition of 'two or more' means a list containing at least two members, and thus requires a list of the form:

```
(X1 X2 | X3)
```

Here, the first part specifically includes two members, and no list of less than two members fits this pattern. X3 is the tail, and this can include any number – including zero. In other words, it can be empty, and this is crucial. Thus any list of two or more members will match this pattern. The statement 'do not like two or more people' therefore becomes:

```
not like a list of the form (X1 X2 | X3)
```

We know that Sue is such a person. We could start by defining unsociable as:

```
(X unsociable if X likes Y & not Y EQ (X1 X2 | X3))
```

The first query condition ensures that Y is generated for checking by the negated EQ condition. The database will be scanned for X and Y candidates, and when a pair is found, Y is matched up to (X1 X2| X3) to see whether it has two or more members. If not, then X is a solution. Backtracking then occurs to return to the database and find more occurrences.

If you try the above, and use 'all' to query it, Sue will be the only result. However, this is a restricted set of answers. How about all the other people who are not mentioned as specifically liking anyone in particular? For instance, look at the database and you will see that Harry likes no one at all – surely he should be called unsociable, to say the least! The form of the above relation only generates those people who are mentioned in the 'likes' part of the database. To include absolutely everyone, you will have to include all persons. This means using the 'person' relation, instead of restricting to the 'likes' relation for the candidate generation in the 'unsociable' definition.

There are several ways to include the missing people, and one way is to think of the definition of 'unsociable' in parts. The first part could be as above. The second part could simply be a check for persons who do not specifically like anyone. This latter could be written:

```
(X unsociable if X person & not X likes Y)
```

The 'person' relation generates all people, and each is then checked to see whether it participates in the 'likes' relation. If there is no such example, then this X forms one of the answers. This finally produces all the required people.

The last part of this definition is quite complex; it involves a complete nested search of the database. For each candidate value of X which is passed onto the 'not likes' part, the whole database has to be searched from top to bottom to confirm that X does not like anyone. If during this search any value is found for Y, then this particular check fails, and the process backtracks without an answer to print.

More complex relations can be negated by using brackets to surround the extent of the negation. For instance, an 'or' construction can be negated as follows:

```
(X non-person if not(either X male or X female))
```

This will have no solutions in this particular database. In addition, it cannot be used to generate non-persons. The 'not' relation cannot be used as a generator, only as a checker.

Brackets must always be used around complex conditions which are to be negated.

*Example 3.7*

(a) Use 'or' to construct a query which finds all the people who like zero or four people.

(b) Define a relation called 'zero-or-positive' which checks whether a number is greater than zero.

(c) Define the 'antisocial' relation, similar to the 'unsociable' relation, but such that a person is defined as antisocial if he or she likes no one at all. How could you redefine 'unsociable' using the 'antisocial' relation?

(d) How would you query the database to find all those people who like males? Can you extend this to finding all those people who do not like males?

(e) Use negation to define 'female' from 'male'. Explain how the use of this definition would differ from that of the existing definition of 'female' on the database.

## Summary

**SUM(X Y Z)** Equivalent to X + Y = Z. SUM can have at most one unknown argument for micro-PROLOG to find. If there are no unknowns, it is used to check the truth of an addition statement.

**TIMES(X Y Z)** Equivalent to X * Y = Z. TIMES can also take at most one unknown argument, and, again, can be used for checking.

**numbers** These can be integers from −32767 to 32767, or floating point numbers with 8 digits of accuracy. Bare minus signs, and decimal points, may not be used without a leading digit, and plus signs are not needed, or allowed, to denote that a number is positive. Overflow in the number of digits which a number can have automatically causes the exponential 'E' notation to be used.

**LESS** This numeric binary relation is true if its first argument is strictly less than its second. It cannot be used to generate numbers.

**EQ** This binary relation is used to check that two objects are equal, or to generate an object equal to another.

**INT** In unary form, this relation simply gives a true answer if its argument is an integer. In binary form, the second argument must always be an unknown variable. INT then sets this unknown to the integer part of the value of its first argument. This integer part is always rounded downwards, even if negative. INT cannot be used to check that a given value is the integer part of another given value.

**Programming** This process should always be started by giving a name to a function or relation, and then considering the required arguments. The routine for the process may then require the definition of further relations, and the addition of rules for those relations on the database.

**list** This is a set of objects of any type which are separated by spaces, and contained within round brackets.

**sublist** The objects within a list may include other lists. These lists, contained within a list, are called sublists.

**singleton** This is a list containing just one member. Note that the single member may be a sublist, and hence contain many further objects.

**empty list** This list contains no members, and is written as ().

**head** This is the extreme left-hand member of a list. It may itself be a sublist.

**tail** This is the whole list minus its head.

**followed by** This relation is represented by a vertical bar, and allows a general list pattern to be constructed with an explicit form of head. Thus, (X | Y) implies that the head is a single member, while the tail is anything, including the empty list.

**(either ... or ... )** This is a method of 'oring' rules or queries together. It is useful in simplifying queries, but is not necessary, or even advisable, in the construction of rules. It is often neater and more easily understood to store several rules on the database, rather than oring them together in a complicated single rule. The effect will be the same.

**not** This is a unary relation for negating a rule or relation. It cannot be used to generate values, only to check them.

## Solutions to problems

*Example 3.1*

(a)
```
(tri-mult(X1 X2 X3 Z)
          if TIMES(X1 X2 Y) & TIMES(X3 Y Z))
```

This function will fail if one of the first two arguments is left as the unknown, because Y in the first TIMES is unknown anyway, and if X1 or X2 is also unknown, this TIMES function has too many unknowns. Either, but only one, of the other two variables may be unknown, because they only appear in the second TIMES, by which time Y has been calculated. If X3 is unknown, for instance, Z will be known, as will Y, and the second TIMES will succeed in finding X3.

(b) The definition required is:

```
(backdiv(X Y Z) if TIMES(X Z Y))
```

This is fully reversible, because TIMES is.

(c) The definition required is:

```
(X inverse-of Y  if  TIMES(X Y 1))
```

and it is fully reversible.

(d) A reasonable definition of SQRT-OF might appear to be:

```
(X SQRT-OF Y if TIMES(X X Y))
```

However, this cannot work as micro-PROLOG would have to generate an infinite series of answers for X until it found two which would multiply together to give Y. This will work the other way around, of course, to find Y – the square of a number given the value of X.

*Example 3.2*

(a) The other two are greater-than and greater-than-or-equal. These will be abbreviated to GRTR and GRTREQ. Their definitions use the three relations given above as follows:

```
(X GRTR Y if Y LESS X)
```

and

```
(X GRTREQ Y if Y LESSEQ X)
```

(b) The definition of LESSEQ consists of two sentences. The first uses LESS, and will immediately fail if given the variable X, with unknown value. However, the second sentence uses EQ, and if it is placed on the database first, it will actually generate the answer 4 before backtracking looks to the next sentence for further answers and fails.

(c) The second rule for LESSEQ simply says that X is LESSEQ to anything equal to itself. This can be expressed succintly by storing the following simple fact on the database:

```
(X LESSEQ X)
```

This gives a neat replacement for the second rule of LESSEQ.

*Example 3.3*

(a) X is between Y and Z if Y is less than X, and X is less than Z:

```
(between(Y X Z) if Y LESS X & X LESS Z)
```

If X can equal one of the bounds, then the following will define within-range:

```
(within-range(Y X Z) if Y LESSEQ X & X LESSEQ Z)
(X LESSEQ Y if X LESS Y)
(X LESSEQ X)
```

All of these definitions will have to be on the database for the within-range function to work. When the program is called up, LESSEQ is checked by using the second or third definition above.

Neither of the relations above can be used to generate numbers, for the same reasons that LESS cannot.

(b) The cube of a number is the result of multiplying the number by itself three times. To write a program, we must select a relation name. We will call it cube1000. It only needs a single argument, which is the given number. The routine is to cube the given number and compare it to 1000. The complete definition is:

(X cube1000 if TIMES(X X Y) & TIMES (X Y Z) & Z LESS 1000)

This relation can only be queried for a true or a false answer; it cannot be used to generate numbers with cubes less than 1000.

*Example 3.4*

To store this routine for later use, we need to rewrite it as a rule, using an 'if'. Following the programming method described earlier, the first step is to choose a name, and define the arguments of the relation. We will call it 'apple-buy', and assume that the price of apples and the amount of money available have to be input. The output arguments will be the number of apples, and the amount left over. Thus the relation has four arguments, two input, and two output. It will be written as:

```
apple-buy(X1 X2 Y1 Y2)
```

where X1 and X2 are the inputs – the price of apples, and the amount available respectively. Y1 and Y2 are the outputs – the number of apples and the amount left over respectively.

The routine defining the relation is the same as in the query given above. Thus the final rule would be added to the database by:

```
add(apple-buy(X1 X2 Y1 Y2) if TIMES(Z1 X1 X2) & Z1 INT Y1
    & TIMES(Y1 X1 Z2) & SUM(Y2 Z2 X2))
```

This is a little involved, but if you compare it carefully you will see that it achieves the same effect as the query routine. The variable names cause the greatest problem as there is no way of using more mnemonic-sounding variables as in BASIC.

Its use would be as follows:

```
which(no. apples = X
          and amount left over = Y : apple-buy(17 75 X Y))
```

You should try this out, and then insert some other numbers of your own to check that you are familiar with this query. You should also try using the relation in reverse, and using it to check the truth of a statement. In this way you will find the limitations of the program. You should try to understand why it fails or succeeds as you experiment with it.

*Example 3.5*

(a) The tails are (Paul Harry) and (Pam Sue). The query would be:

all((X1 X2):John likes (X X1 X2))

(b) (i) A (ii) (A B) (iii) () the empty list.
(c) (i) (D E) (ii) () the empty list (iii) ((A) B)

*Example 3.6*

(a) The pattern for the third member of any list relies upon that list having at least three members. Thus, the pattern:

```
(X1 X2 X3 | X4)
```

ensures that the list searched for has three members, and of course X3 is the required third member. Thus, the query program would be:

```
all(X3 : Y likes (X1 X2 X3 | X4))
```

This is purely a query, and is lost when executed. It could be stored using:

```
add(X3 third-member if Y likes (X1 X2 X3 | X4))
```

(b) This kind of query always takes a little thought to sort out. It is worth looking at the database to ensure that the conditions are clear. The translation to a micro-PROLOG query is fairly straightforward, if a little involved. The routine will be to find a list liked by Mary, isolate its head, check whether it is male and if so find the people liked by that person. The query is:

```
all(X:Mary likes (X1 | X2) & X1 male & X1 likes X)
```

The head of the males liked by Mary is John, and he likes (George Paul Harry) and (Mary Pam Sue).

The same is constructed for George, but the final answer is the empty set, because Paul does not specifically like anyone. micro-PROLOG will answer

'No (more) answers'; it will not print out the empty set as ().

(c) Again, this is simply a question of sorting out the words. Mary and John each like a separate list of females, and the tails of these lists are to be formed into a single list. A pattern must be found for the final answer, and the constituents of the pattern generated. The pattern being searched for is:

(X Y) where X and Y are tails of other lists

This translates to:

```
all((X Y):Mary likes (X1 | X) & X1 female
        & John likes (X2 | Y) & X2 female)
```

This satisfies the conditions correctly, and certainly gives a printout of the required lists, held in a new list. This only works correctly because Mary and John each like just one list of females, and thus the final list only contains two tails X and Y. Recursion is required for more general cases. The answer, with the database shown previously, will be:

```
((Pam) (Pam Sue))
```

This is a slightly different list form from the others in that it contains two sublists. This is only to be expected as it comes from a pattern containing two lists X and Y. However, there are many cases where we want the answer to be a list of members all on the same level within the main list, and this can only be achieved by taking the sublists apart and storing the individual members onto a third list. We cannot do this yet, but this is the type of list manipulation which is common in list-processing languages, and we shall see how to do it in the next chapter.

(d) The tail of the tail is found by stripping the head off the list twice. In other words, remove the first two members by matching the list with the pattern:

```
(X1 X2 | Z)
```

where Z is the tail of the tail. This will only work if the original list has two or more members.

The query required is:

```
all(Z:(A (B C D) E F) EQ (X1 X2 | Z))
```

This will yield the answer (E F), by simple pattern matching. Note that the first two members of the constant list are A and (B C D).

*Example 3.7*

(a) The query is:

```
all(X:(either X person & not X likes Y
           or X likes (X1 X2 X3 X4)))
```

(b) A definition is:

```
(X zero-or-positive if (either X EQ 0 or 0 LESS X))
```

Note that '0 LESS X' is used to define the condition that X is to be positive and not zero.

(c) The 'antisocial' relation is identical to the second definition of the 'unsociable' relation. That definition was constructed to find all those people who did not specifically like anyone. The definition is:

```
(X antisocial if X person & not X likes Y)
```

The 'unsociable' relation could be written:

```
(X unsociable if X likes Y & not Y EQ (X1 X2 | X3))
(X unsociable if X antisocial)
```

This is complex enough to be stored as two separate conditions on the database rather than trying to type in a long 'or' expression.

(d) To query the database we could simply construct an 'is' function, but this would not store the definition on the database for future use. We will define a relation so that it can be stored.

If you look at the database, we have carefully included only people of one sex within each list after the 'likes' relation. This means that we only have to check the head of a list liked by someone to see whether they like males or not. We will meet ways of solving the case where all members of a list have to be checked in the next chapter.

To ensure that we find everyone, we need only look at those people who like someone, and then check to see whether the list they like is male or female. We will call this function 'likes-males', and it can be written as:

```
(X likes-males if X likes (X1 | X2) & X1 male)
```

This starts by generating X, X1 and X2. Forward tracking then passes X1 onto the male relation. If X1 is male, X is printed as a solution. Backtracking then returns micro-PROLOG to the start of the routine, and 'likes' is used to continue the search in the database for more candidates to be checked.

To find those people who do not like males, we have to think carefully of all those classes of people who are to be included. We must include those who like just females, and those who like no one. It is once again crucial to include the whole set. People who do not like anyone are covered by the definition of 'antisocial' and this forms part of the definition of 'not-likes-males' which we will be defining. Thus:

```
(X not-likes-males if X antisocial)
```

The next part requires all those people who like females, and not males. We can use the negative of the definition of likes-males to check that any people we generate as candidates do not like males. Thus the next part of the definition is:

```
(X not-likes-males if X likes Y & not X likes-males)
```

This completes the definition. Once again, the last part of this definition involves an entire nested search of the database from the top in order to check that X likes-males is not true. Once again, also, two separate definitions are preferable to a single complicated 'or' construction.

(e) The female relation can be defined as:

```
(X female if not X male)
```

This can certainly be used to check whether a person is female or not, assuming that male and female between them covers all the objects on the database. If other nouns were stored there in the rules, this definition would treat anything not defined as 'male' to be female.

The definition above cannot be used to generate female names. If used as a generator, micro-PROLOG will have to start looking around for all the 'non-males' in the universe to solve the problem.

## Chapter Four

# Recursion, and Further Programming Techniques

### Introduction

The information presented so far will have given you a good grounding in the main principles and keywords offered by the SIMPLE front-end processor of micro-PROLOG. We will see later how to transfer this into the underlying code of the language, if you wish to take the language further. This chapter stays with SIMPLE, and introduces an important programming technique called *recursion*. It is sufficiently important to occupy most of the chapter, though some other facilities are also introduced here to allow the examples to be as comprehensive as possible.

Recursion is one of the more problematic programming concepts in computing, and this stems from what may be seen as a rather awkward way of looking at logic, and using it to produce some quite dramatic effects. It is difficult to describe the great advantages which recursion gives you until you have seen it at work, and tried it out for yourself. Without recursion, much of AI would be difficult, if not impossible. This stems largely from the crucial importance recursion has for general list processing. However, recursion is based on mathematics, logic and the use of numbers. If you were interested in number theory, for instance, recursion, or similar techniques, would be fundamental to most of your work.

### The failure of previous techniques

So far we have carefully skirted around the problems of generalising the examples given in the last chapter. For instance, the last chapter used a database of lists of people liked by other people. We ensured that the examples worked by keeping females and males separately listed. If the lists had been combined, it would have been difficult, for instance, to find out which males a given person liked. Let us look at this type of example, and see where the problems occur.

To follow this example, you will have to start from a clean slate, and input the following facts:

```
Mary likes (John Harry George)
Sue likes (George Mary Pam Paul)
Paul likes (George Mary Sue)
Pam likes (Mary)
Mary likes (George Sue Pam John Mary)
John likes (Pam John Harry George Mary)
Mary female
Pam female
Sue female
John male
Harry male
George male
Paul male
```

The lists now contain a random selection of males and females, and there is no structure to rely on within the lists. It is even possible for someone to like more than one list, and these lists may overlap. Some people can even be observed liking themselves!

Before, we could find all the males which Mary liked simply by finding an X such that Mary likes X, and X has a head which is male. If Mary liked more than one list of males, this would still find them all. Now that we have removed the condition that a list only contains males, the task becomes more difficult. We now have to examine each member of X, instead of just the head, and print each male which is found.

You have learned to take lists apart, and it is possible to examine each member of a list of, say, four members, and print out all the males. If you know that Mary likes a list of four members, this piece of information will allow you to query for the males in the list as follows:

```
all(Mary likes X1 : Mary likes (X1 X2 X3 X4) & X1 male)
all(Mary likes X2 : Mary likes (X1 X2 X3 X4) & X2 male)
 . . . . . . . and so on.
```

However, this is most awkward. An interative method which simply looks along the list, and examines each member separately is required.

The real problem arises when you have no idea of the size of the list Mary likes. Under these circumstances, no general pattern can be constructed for the complete set of members of the list, and the method fails totally.

Other types of question cannot even be asked yet. For instance, how can you find out how many people Mary likes, or how many people are liked by at most two other people, and so on. These questions involve finding how many members there are in a list, or how many with certain attributes. All this is a problem of list processing, and using some type of counting mechanism. We have no way of doing this so far.

Recursion allows the type of general question posed above to be answered, and allows for counting mechanisms in the solution to conditional questions, and query conditions. It effectively tricks the computer into looping, as we shall see.

Before looking at recursion itself, let us consider the type of loops which would be of use in processing lists. There is one particular procedure which is very important, and it is illustrated next.

## Iteration and general list processing

The concept described above is known as *iteration*, which means, broadly, repetition or looping. micro-PROLOG has no formal loop statement as in most other languages. Instead, it relies entirely on recursion to perform a process repetitively until a given end is reached, or a given answer is built up.

An example of a general iteration is shown in the flow chart of Figure 4.1. This gives a method of finding all the males whom Mary likes, whether or not the sizes of the lists she likes are known. It uses a list processing method which starts by finding a list Y such that Mary likes Y. This list is then examined to see if its head is male, by matching up with the list (X| Z), as before. If X is male, it is printed as one of the answers. The next step is the crucial one – it takes the tail, Z, and sets Y equal to this tail. This effectively strips the head off Y, and leaves just the tail.

If Y is not empty, the process is repeated on the new Y, and again its head is examined, and then stripped off. When Y is finally emptied, backtracking occurs to the database to find another Y to be processed in the same way. If another Y cannot be found, the process naturally ends.

This example is not just a single isolated case to illustrate iteration. It is one of the most important methods of processing a list which exists. You will see this method of examining and stripping the head off a list throughout list processing. It is a very straightforward and sequential method of approaching lists – starting at the top, and working down one member at a time. You should always consider this approach when you have any list processing to perform. There are variations, of course, but you will see the fundamental idea represented again and again.

As another example of the process, let us find the lengths of the lists which Mary likes. There may be several such lists, and it may be important to know the length of each one.

Figure 4.2 shows how to program this example. Again, a Y is found which Mary likes, but this time the counter X1 is zeroed, as this is the numerical variable which will hold the answer. Again, the list's head is stripped off, but no examination takes place. The counter X1 is simply incremented to make a count of the number of heads which are stripped off the list. If Y is not yet empty, the process of head stripping is repeated, counting all the time, until Y is empty. At that point, X1 is printed as the answer, and backtracking occurs, and either the process is at an end, or the next Y on the database is found.

This illustrates once again how useful the sequential process of dealing with successive heads in the list can be. It suggests that when there is a

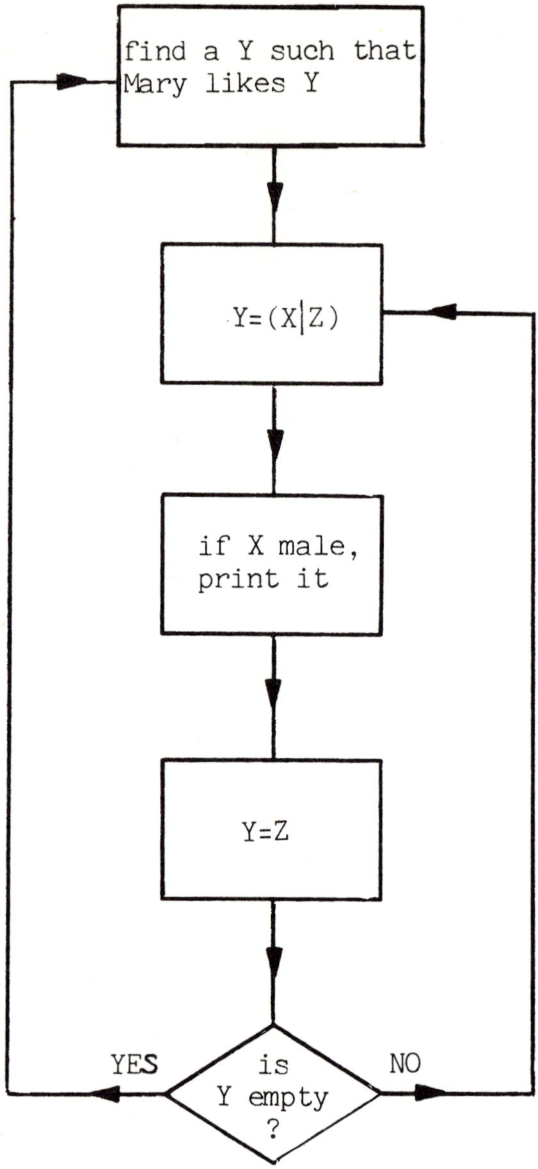


*Figure 4.1.* Finding the males liked by Mary.

process to perform on a list, the list should be considered as a series of heads of smaller and smaller sublists.

The problem is to make micro-PROLOG perform iteration. To see how to do this, we will now look at recursion in detail, and return to the above examples later.

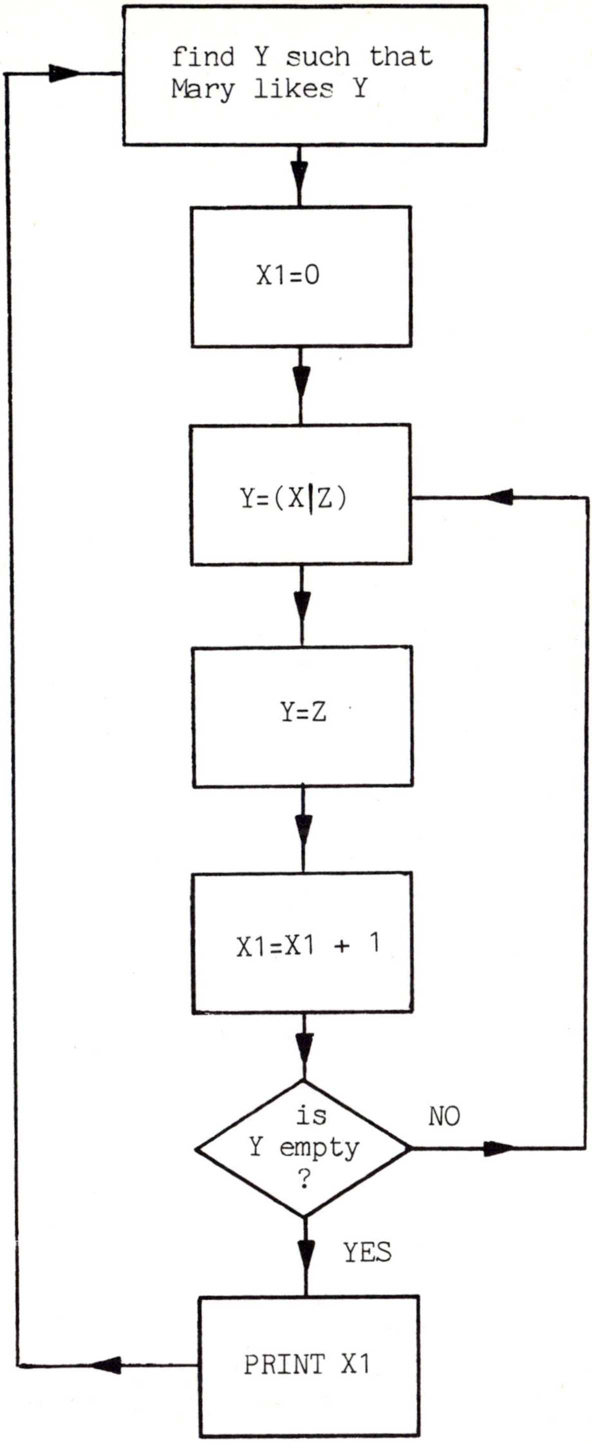


*Figure 4.2.* Finding the number of people liked by Mary.

## Recursion

Recursion is the method of using a definition to define itself. This awkward circularity is at the root of most problems which people have when seeing this concept for the first time. To see how to do it, consider the following two definitions of a list:

(1) *A list is a set of objects including constants and variables, separated by spaces, and contained within round brackets.*
(2) *A list is a set of objects including constants, variables and lists, separated by spaces, and contained within round brackets.*

The difference is purely that the second definition includes lists as allowable objects within lists. It effectively uses the concept of a list to assist in defining itself, and hence is a recursive definition. This has a profound effect on the objects generated by the definition, and looking at these objects will give you an idea as to why recursion causes iteration.

To see the effect of the recursion, let us first consider all the objects generated by the first definition. Examples of such objects would be:

(915.678) () (A B C) (X Y X1 Hello 23.3) (1 2 3 4 5 0)

and so on. Each example here is a (possibly empty) list of single non-list objects, and only has one pair of round brackets – the ones around the list. No other type of structure will be generated by definition (1), and these examples are actually quite general.

Definition (2) will include all of the above examples, but it also allows the list to contain other lists. Thus, an example would be:

(A B C (1 2 3) 4 5 6)

Here, the list contains a number of normal objects plus a single list. However, the definition says that a list can contain lists, and thus the sublist above, being a list, can itself contain a list. This might give:

(A B C (1 2 (X Y Z) 3) 4 5 6)

This gives two nested lists within the main list. This process can continue because the inner sublist, being a list, can contain further lists, and so on.

To give some idea of the hierarchies of lists which the second definition generates, the following gives just three types:

```
((A))             ((A) (B))           ((A) (B) (C))
((A B))           ((A B) (C D))       ((A B) (C D) (E F))
((A) (B C))       ((A) (B) (C D))     ((A) (B) (C) (D E))
```

and so on.

The addition of lists of lists allows an infinite sequence of infinite sequences of lists and sublists to be generated from the definition. These sequences are impossible to write down fully. The first line above is the start of the sequence of lists containing just singletons as members. The second line shows lists containing just doubletons (2-member lists). The third line shows how the singletons and doubletons can mix together. This process of generating all possible list types, even for just singletons and doubletons, can never be written down fully! Then we have to consider lists containing hierarchies of sublists such as:

((((A (B (C (D) E) F) G) H) I) J)

This is quite a complex list to human beings, but to the recursive definition, it is hardly even the start of the process!

As you can see, simply by adding in the extra word 'lists' to be included in the definition (1) above, a complex iteration of different list types is suddenly included. It is a common effect of recursion that the addition of a simple recursive condition produces a whole repetition of values automatically.

To illustrate the effect of recursion causing iteration, there is a famous story by Larry Niven of a problem set by a demon conjured up during an experiment into the black arts. The demon laconically announces that the experimenter is doomed, and that within 24 hours he will be spirited away to Hell forever. In return, the man is granted one wish. When the 24 hours are up, the demon will return, but if the man has drawn a pentagram anywhere, of any size, the demon will be forced to jump into it. The demon explains, however, that this will not stop him from sealing the man's fate.

After a moment's thought, the man asks for time to be stopped for everything but himself. His single wish is granted, and the whole world, including the demon, is frozen for a 24 hour period. The man then carefully draws his pentagram, and fearfully awaits the period's ending.

When time begins moving again, the demon returns to consciousness, and is forced to jump into the pentagram which the man has drawn – on the demon's own chest!

As the demon jumps into the pentagram on his own chest, he reduces in size to fit in, and takes the pentagram with him. He is thus forced to jump into that smaller pentagram. The process successfully repeats itself, and the demon is reduced to non-existence, thus freeing the man from his unimaginable fate!

This is a direct application of recursion. The demon's body had to jump to an area within his own body, thus reducing the size of the pentagram for the next jump and so on. A single definitive act by the experimenter caused a large series of subsequent acts to occur automatically. In this case, the recursion had no ending, and the loop was thus infinite. In general, you will see that an ending must be included within the recursion, as for any other type of loop.

## Recursion in practice

The above provides an introduction to the principle of recursion, but does not yet explain how to invoke it in micro-PROLOG. As you may have guessed, there are no special keywords involved, it is simply a question of gaining an understanding of the logical statements required for a recursion, and writing them as micro-PROLOG rules. In fact, the rule for invoking recursion is simple enough – a function is said to use recursion if it calls itself within its own definition.

We will now look at a simple example which uses recursion, and thus learn how to make the computer iterate automatically.

Suppose that we wish to find every list which contains just males. As the lists contain random people, each one has to be scanned fully to ensure that it contains no females.

As with all micro-PROLOG programs, the first step is to think of a name for the relation being constructed, and define the arguments which will be used. This is particularly important in recursion, as when the definition refers back to itself, it will need to use a name for the call.

The relation we will define will look like this:

```
X all-male
```

It is a unary relation, and X is any list.

The approach to this problem will be to use the head stripping procedure. The head of X is examined first. If it is not male, the list cannot be all male, and the answer to a query would be NO (see Figure 4.3). If the head is male, then the tail of the list must be looked at. This is done by setting X to its own tail, and sending it around the loop again. However, it is important to stop the process if X is empty, because this means that no females have been found, and YES is the answer to the query. The process continues until either the list has been fully examined, and X is empty, or a single female is found.

You should now read carefully through the following logic as it will help you to understand the reasons behind the process, and thus give you the ability to invent your own procedures in due course.

The main iterative part of the process in Figure 4.3 is to examine X's head, and then use the all-male relation on X's tail. This can be translated into:

```
X all-male if:
X EQ (X1 | X2) & X1 male & X2 all-male
```

In other words, a list is all-male if its head and its tail are all male. This may seem obvious, but it is this simple statement which produces the iteration in the program. micro-PROLOG will start by matching X up with a pattern identifying the head, X1, and the tail, X2, separately. The head is checked, and if not male the process stops there, and gives the answer NO, as this value of X is clearly not all-male. If X's head is male, forward tracking causes

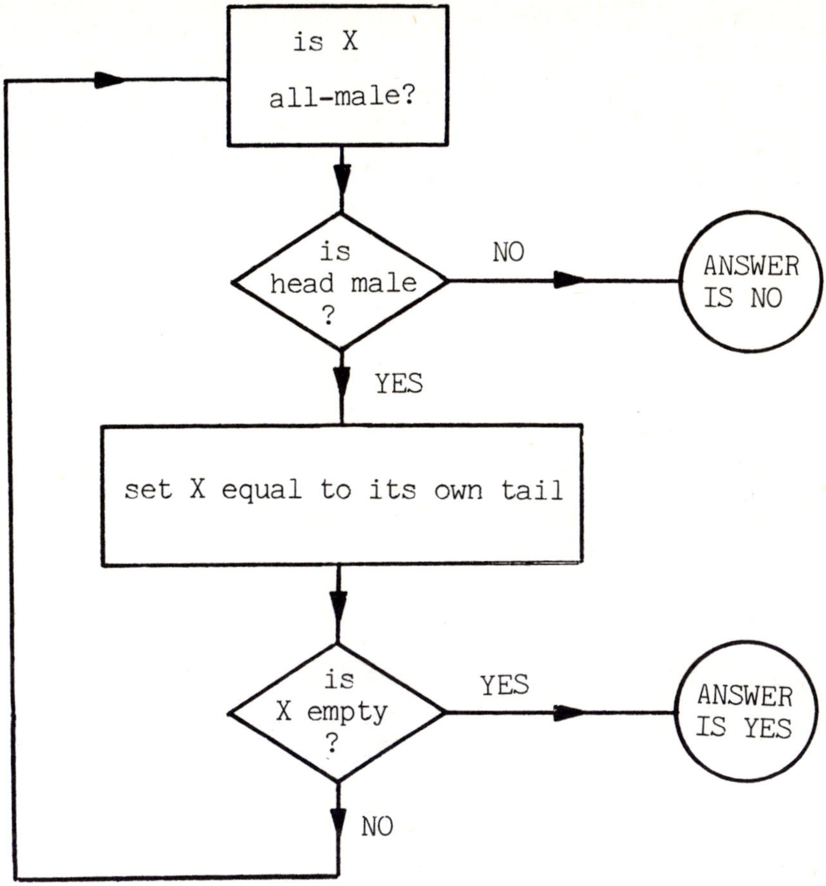


*Figure 4.3.* All-male recursion.

the tail of X to be examined to see whether it is all-male. If it is ultimately found to be so, then X must be. It is this recursive use of the all-male relation within the definition which causes the looping. The process repeats on the tail of X, and then on the tail of that tail, and so on. This process continues automatically simply because the definition is circular. Unfortunately, the process is rather too circular, and there is no graceful exit! The only way in which the process can end is by the tail eventually becoming empty. At that point, the pattern (X1 | X2) simply does not match up to the tail, and an error is signalled. Thus, the process is not allowed to reach its correct conclusion. We must now add in the mechanism for ending the loop. The process of backtracking will then occur to find the rest of the answers.

To do this, we will add an extra condition at the start of the definition. There is normally more than one method of ending such a process. Each time all-male is called up, the list could be checked to see if it is empty before allowing it to run headlong into the recursion, and an error. We could simply add in an extra rule for the all-male relation which says that a list is all-male if it is empty. This may seem strange, but it ensures that if the whole process has managed to make it far enough to empty the list, without encountering any females, the list must be all-male. The final definition, therefore, could be written informally as follows:

```
X all-male  if:
either X EQ ()
or X EQ (X1 | X2) & X1 male & X2 all-male
```

Another way to ensure a proper ending would be to examine the given list to see if it is a singleton male. Such a list is certainly all-male, and this form also ultimately occurs as a result of the head-stripping recursive procedure. This would give a definition as follows:

```
X all-male  if:
either X EQ (X1) & X1 male
or X EQ (X1 | X2) & X1 male & X2 all-male
```

Either of the two definitions above will work, but the second is perhaps more obviously meaningful, and perhaps a little more efficient. If X is a singleton male from the start, the recursion is never entered, which makes for a faster answer in such a case.

The latter definition highlights two very important points about micro-PROLOG. First, note how X1 is used in both the second and the third lines of the rule, probably with different values in each. There is no conflict here as it is given a specific value by each line in which it appears. Second, the rules above give a very general format for a recursive definition. There is usually a condition at the beginning which causes the recursion to stop, or perhaps never start under some circumstances. This is followed by the recursion itself. These two components can be considerably more complex than is shown here, but the essence of the pattern is generally preserved.

The above definitions can be placed on the database in one of two ways. The (either ... or ... ) method could be used, or two separate definitions could be stored. The latter produces a slightly more easily understood and more easily edited version, as follows:

```
X all-male if X EQ (X1) & X1 male
X all-male if X EQ (X1 | X2) & X1 male & X2 all-male
```

This will work perfectly, and the next section tells you how to use the definition. However, there is one further note which should be made at this point, which is one of programming style as much as anything. The above uses the EQ relation to match a given X with a list of the form (X1) or (X1| X2). This was chosen to make the operations clear, but it is not the best style to adopt, and the definitions can be shortened by a simple trick.

When the definition is used, micro-PROLOG will start by matching a given list with X – in other words, X will be given a value. This value is then matched up with a list form using EQ. These two matches can be done in a single operation simply by rewriting the definition as follows:

```
(X1) all-male if X1 male
(X1 | X2) all-male if X1 male & X2 all-male
```

Thus, a given list value is matched up immediately with (X1) or (X1 | X2), and there is no need for the intermediate step. Furthermore, using the empty condition given before, an even more compact definition would be:

```
() all-male
(X1 | X2) all-male if X1 male & X2 all-male
```

However, you should be clear that these two definitions are not exactly equal as they treat the empty set differently. In the following, we will use the first of these two definitions, and thus always assume that the list is checked to see if it is a singleton male before appealing to the recursion.

## Using the recursion

This relation can only be used to check that a given list is all-male, it cannot be used to generate all-male lists. Thus, to use the relation, it must either be queried directly for a given value, or it must be placed in a query containing a generating function before the all-male relation is used. We will now look at both of these types of example.

If you have loaded the database suggested above, your machine will contain statements about which people are male, and which female. If you now construct a list of people, a normal query should be able to use the all-male relation to find out whether it is all-male or not. For example:

```
is((George Paul Harry) all-male)
```

The above rules will start by checking whether the given list is a male singleton, which it is not. The next step is to strip the heads off the sublists, and examine each to see whether it is male or not. As each one is male, until a singleton male is reached, the answer is YES.

The following example gives NO:

```
is((George Paul Pam) all-male)
```

This shows how to use the relation for explicit lists. We will now find all the all-male lists on the database. To do this, a generating function must be used to produce all the lists, and each one will have to be checked. The 'likes' relation will generate all the lists, and pass them on to the query condition for checking. The following will achieve the aim, with a comment to help in the legibility of the answer:

```
all(X are all male:Y likes X & X all-male)
```

If you have typed in the database suggested, the only answer to this will be:

```
(John Harry George)
```

*Example 4.1*
(a) Write down the answers to:

(i) is(() all-male)
(ii) is((Paul George) all-male)
(iii) is(Paul all-male)

(b) Construct a definition of the relation 'sociable-list' which gives an affirmative answer when presented with a list of people, each of whom likes someone else in the database. Give two examples of the use of this relation, one for an explicit list of people where the relation succeeds, and one to find all the lists on the database which satisfy the relation.

## Following the recursion through

To construct your own recursions in general, it is important to have an understanding of the underlying process. It is important, for instance, to realise that while a recursion loop is running, it is stacking operations away for later execution. This stacking can use up large quantities of memory, and it is important to use recursion as efficiently as possible. To understand this, we will now look at the recursion in a little more detail.

The best way to describe this concept is to use a simple example, and follow through its working. We will look at the following:

```
is((Paul George Harry) all-male)
```

To make the following explanation a little easier to see, we will go back to the first method of defining all-male as follows:

```
X all-male if X EQ (X1) & X1 male
X all-male if X EQ (X1 | X2) & X1 male & X2 all-male
```

There is no difference, except one of programming style, but this definition makes the processes clearer and easier to view.

Figure 4.4 shows the processes which occur as this query is executed. To start with, X in the definition of all-male is set equal to (Paul George Harry). The first part of the definition is then used to see if, by any stroke of luck, X is simply a singleton male. If so, of course, the process would end affirmatively. However, this is not the case here, as shown. X is then matched up with (X1 | X2), and as X1 is male, X2 is checked to see if it is all-male. If so, again the process ends in the affirmative. However, this cannot be decided just yet, as X2 must now be plugged into the all-male definition to see whether it is all-male. This means that until this is done, the decision about X2 must remain pending, until fully checked. The next part of the diagram shows this value of X2 being checked by appealing to the definition of all-male again – with X equal to this X2, which is (George Harry), being the tail of the original value of X.

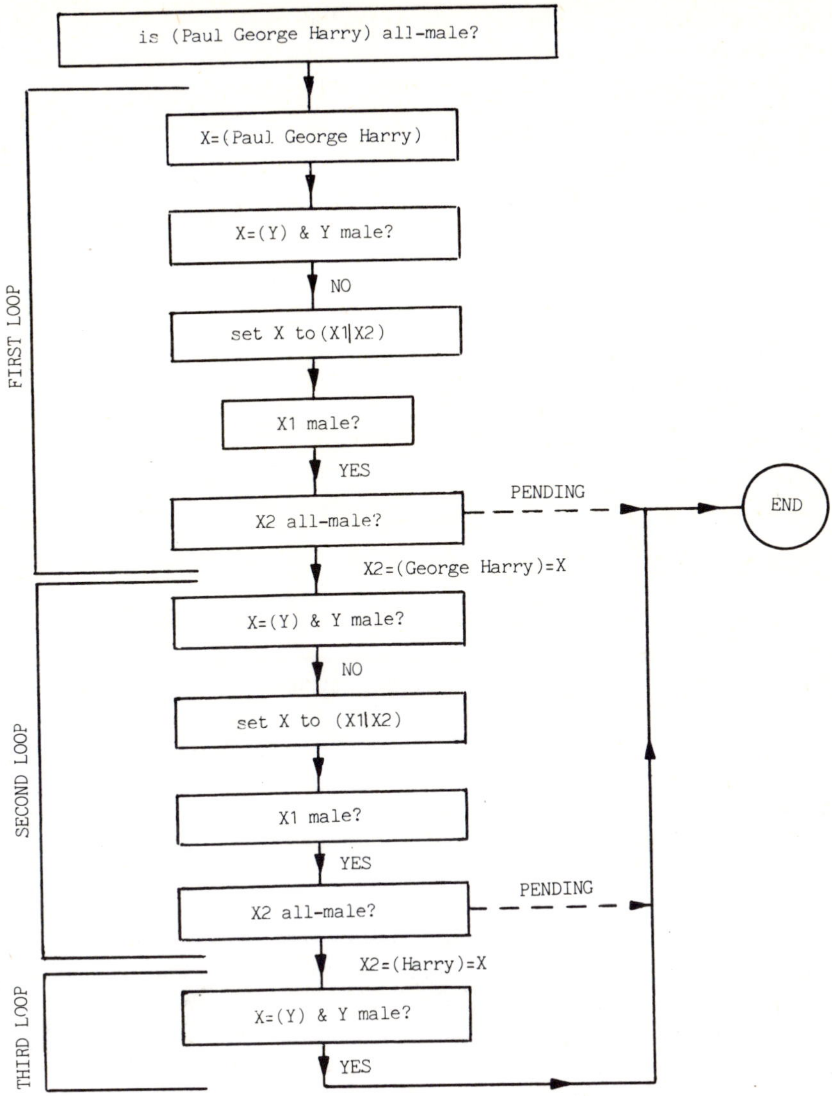


*Figure 4.4.* Pending operations in recursion.

This second use of all-male forms the second loop in the process, and you should remember that the outcome of this application of all-male will decide the previously pending logical decision.

This second loop follows the first exactly, and even produces a further, nested, pending decision, which another application of all-male, in the third loop, decides immediately. This occurs because, by then, the value of X is a singleton male, and there is no problem in deciding the all-male question without resorting to a further recursion.

Now that the final loop solves the second pending decision, and this solves the first one, micro-PROLOG simply combines all these affirmatives, shown by the solid line working its way back up the diagram. The final answer, therefore, is YES.

If any females had been found, the process would have stopped immediately, and given a NO.

As you can see, if you have more members in the initial list, more levels will, theoretically, be left pending. The more levels, the more memory is required by micro-PROLOG. If there are too many levels, as might occur in a fairly large recursion, the computer runs out of memory, and the problem cannot be solved.

In addition, if you are querying using 'all', the machine has even more to store, as it may constantly have to remember deeper and deeper levels of backtracking at the same time. This is an important consideration in many applications of recursion. However, micro-PROLOG helps to solve this problem by a concept called *tail-recursion.*

## Tail-recursion

The simple program shown in Figure 4.4 does not really need a recursion, it can easily be replaced by a single-level loop – that is, a loop which does not need to store all the intermediate pending levels. If you had to solve the problem using BASIC, or if micro-PROLOG offered a looping function instead of relying on recursion, you would use a simple loop, and save memory.

micro-PROLOG is clever enough to detect the cases where a simple loop will do, and where it can rely on a single level of storage, instead of building up masses of nested data. If you simply place the recursion in the last position in the last line of the program, as we have done here, micro-PROLOG automatically uses a single-level storage method to perform the process. This means that quite large lists can be checked without running into this particular memory problem. This is a good reason for learning the habit of placing the ending conditions of a recursion at the start, and the recursion itself at the very end of the set of rules. Hence the expression 'tail-recursion'. The full condition for tail recursion is that the recursive condition must be the last condition in the last rule, for the required definition.

In any dialect of PROLOG which you may encounter, it is always worth finding out whether it provides tail-recursion.

It is often possible to write some recursions in two ways – with and without tail recursion. The only difference, in general, will be the memory efficiency.

## Lengths of lists, and counting

The problem described by Figure 4.2, finding the number of people liked by Mary, involves a recursive counting procedure. This problem is akin to the problem of finding the length of a list. We will look at both of these problems now, starting with the latter.

As with the previous example of looping using recursion, the approach is to trick the program into looping by giving recursive, or circular, rules. It is not normal, using recursion, to set up an initially zero loop counter, and add to it with each head-stripping operation. Rather, an overall circular definition is chosen.

The approach to finding the length of a list is to note that the length equals one more than the length of its tail. Thus, if you can find the length of the tail of a list, you are home and dry. This is a recursive view of the problem, and is a general way of looking at such counting mechanisms. The statement translates into:

```
X length Y if X EQ (X1 | X2) & X2 length Z
              & SUM(Z 1 Y)
```

This starts by matching X with the given list, and then matching X with (X1| X2). The next step is the recursion. The length, Z, of the tail is found, and must be just one less than the final answer, Y, which is expressed by the last condition.

There are several points to note about this definition. First, the recursion will never end because as the head stripping occurs, it will eventually empty the list, and an error will be caused. (We will add the ending condition shortly.) Second, the first part of the definition above can be shortened, as explained before, to remove the EQ. Third, this definition is not tail recursive as the very last condition is not the recursion – it is a SUM.

A neater definition, still not tail-recursive, is:

```
(X1 | X2) length Y if X2 length Z & SUM(Z 1 Y)
```

To end the recursion, we simply allow for the case where the given list becomes empty. If an empty list is given to the 'length' definition, we would expect the outcome to be zero. Thus, the following is the complete pair of rules for the definition:

```
() length 0
(X1 | X2) length Y if X2 length Z & SUM(Z 1 Y)
```

Now, any list which is supplied will be checked to see if it is empty, and if so the answer will be zero without even referring to the recursive part of the definition. Figure 4.5 is a diagram of the process for the following example:

```
all(Y:(A B C D) length Y)
```

This diagram should help you to visualise the process of recursion in general, to aid in the construction of your own recursive definitions.

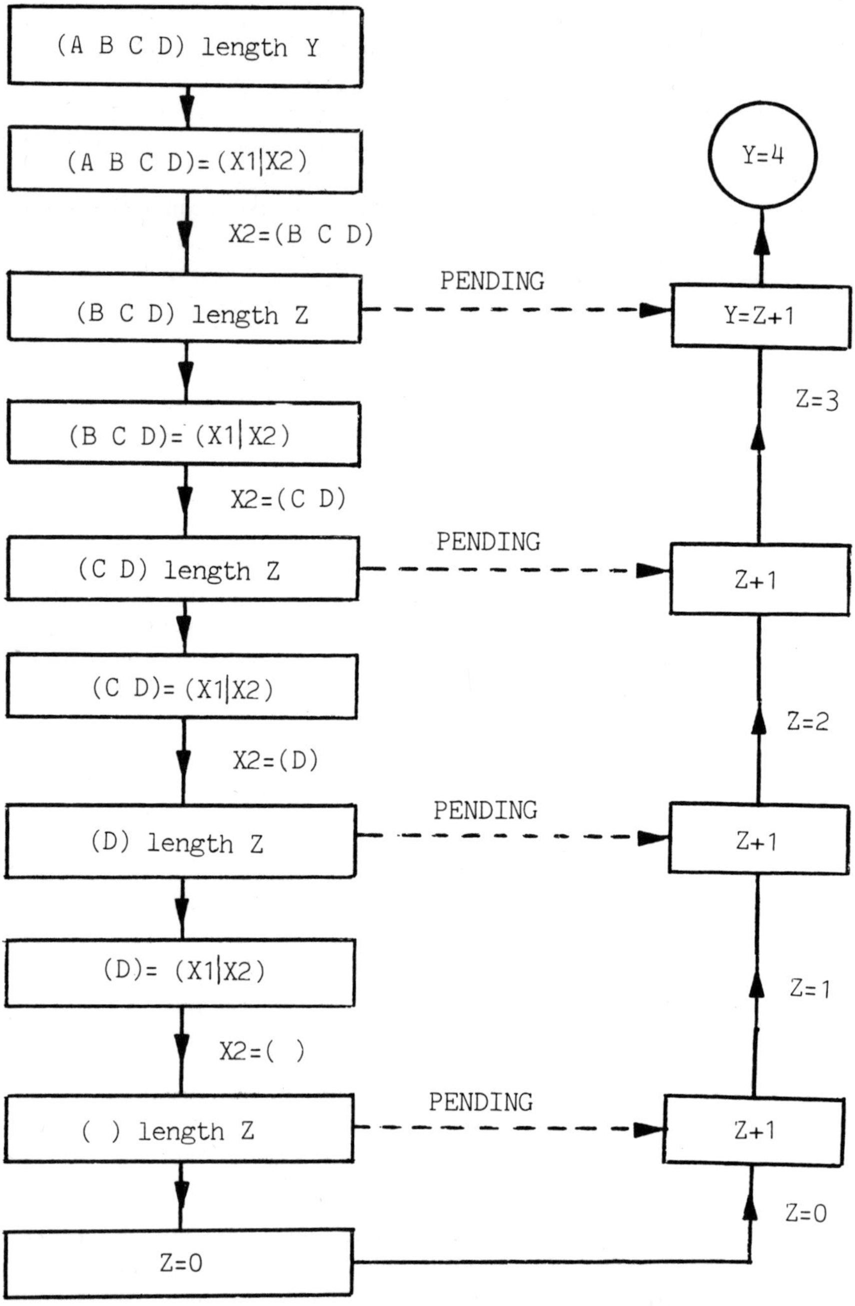


*Figure 4.5.* List length relation.

At the start, (A B C D) is not empty, and is thus matched with (X1 | X2). The length required, Y, is equal to 1 plus the length, Z, of X2, (B C D).

However, this addition cannot be performed until the length of X2 has been found. This causes the addition to wait pending the next level of the use of 'length' on X2.

Moving down the diagram to the next level, this is repeated on (B C D), and then (C D) and so on. Each time, the pending addition waits for the next use of 'length' to be completed before being performed.

When X2 is empty, its length, zero, is given by the first rule in the recursive definition, and the impending additions can then be performed, starting with 1 plus 0, and ending with 4.

As this is not a tail recursion, the number of members of the list does affect the use of memory.

When you have a recursion to define for list processing, remember that you should look for a use of the relation itself to calculate the answer on a list of one less than the given list, and thus cause the definition to loop. You will always have to remember to define an ending rule too. You should be able to see that the ending rule depends upon the recursion mechanism, and where that should normally end.

The next example is to write the program of Figure 4.2 which finds the numbers of people in the sets which Mary likes. This could be done as a stand-alone program as for finding the length of a list above, but it is more easily done using the length function as follows. We will define the relation as 'likes-num', and use it as:

```
X likes-num Y
```

where person X likes a number of people Y. This relation will find the lengths of all lists liked by X. Its definition is as follows:

```
X likes-num Y if X likes Z & Z length Y
```

It can be used to find how many people Mary likes by:

```
all(X:Mary likes-num X)
```

The answers will be 3 and 5. This function does not add the answers together to give a grand total.

## Some arithmetic

Recursion is a very powerful tool in arithmetic, and we will now look at the type of routine which is common in this field. To do this, we will choose an example. The relation required will be to find the sum of all the integers from 0 to X, which is a positive integer. Thus, the answer for X equals 4 would be:

$$0 + 1 + 2 + 3 + 4 = 10$$

The relation defined will be called 'integer-sum', and it has two arguments, one being the given integer, and the other being the answer. Thus, it could be used as:

```
X integer-sum Y
```

where Y is the sum from 0 to X.

The relation simply relies on the fact that the sum from 0 to X is equal to X plus the sum from 0 to X−1. This is a recursive definition. It should end when 0 is reached, and this can be ensured by the rule:

```
0 integer-sum 0
```

The main part of the definition can be written informally as:

```
X integer-sum Y if 0 LESS X & X1 = (X-1)
          & X1 integer-sum Z & Y = Z + X
```

This definition is not applicable if X is zero or negative, and this is excluded by the first part of the definition. Y is then made up by adding the given X to the application of integer-sum to the integer just below X. In this manner, a loop is established which uses lower and lower values of X until 0 is reached. At that point, the process finds an answer to the 'integer-sum' function, and climbs back up the ladder adding the integers as it goes. This eventually produces the answer for Y. The full definition is:

```
0 integer-sum 0
X integer-sum Y if 0 LESS X & SUM(X1 1 X)
                    & X1 integer-sum Z & SUM(Z X Y)
```

This is a general example of the method by which this type of problem is solved.

To use this relation, we could find the sum of all the integers from 0 to 10 by:

```
all(X:10 integer-sum X)
```

The answer is 55. This relation could also be used to check that two numbers satisfy the relation as follows:

```
is(4 integer-sum 10)
```

The answer would be YES. However, the relation cannot be used to find an integer such that the integer-sum equals a given number. In other words, the relation cannot be used to find the inverse. Thus, if you were given 55, you could not generate 10 as X's value above. This is because of the LESS in the definition. If the first argument is unknown, the LESS relation cannot be used to check that 0 is less than the argument, and the relation fails with an error.

To make the integer-sum relation reversible, we will have to replace LESS with a function which actually generates candidates for X which are checked by the remaining two conditions. This means producing a succession of numbers from 0 upwards until the correct number is found. We know that the number is between 0 and the given number, though this is still a wide variation, and requires a large amount of checking.

The extension of integer-sum is left as an exercise in logic.

*Example 4.2*

(1) Show how to use the length relation to find the lengths of all the lists on the current 'likes' database.

(2) Show how to use the 'length' relation to find the number of people in each list on the database which is not liked by a given person. Call the relation 'not-likes-number'. It would be used as follows:

```
all(X:Mary not-likes-number X)
```

(3) Define a recursive relation to find the factorial of the positive integer X. The factorial of a number is the product of all the integers from 2 to X. The factorial of 1 is 1. Give an example of its use.

## The append relation

List processing is not just a question of taking lists apart, it is often necessary to build up, or join lists together. This is still performed member by member using recursion, and we will look at two important relations here.

Appending two lists simply means combining them in a given order – one following the other. For instance, the following two lists:

```
(A B C 6 7 8)    and    (B (5 6) Hello)
```

would append to produce:

```
(A B C 6 7 8 B (5 6) Hello)
```

These have been appended in the order written above, but they might have been appended the other way round. The relation required is called *append.* Its definition is a typical recursive relation. The append relation is used as follows:

```
append(X Y Z)
```

where Z is the append of X onto Y, in that order.

The first rule in the definition of append defines the case where X is empty:

```
append(() Y Y)
```

It should be clear that appending the empty set onto Y leaves it unchanged. The rest of the definition depends upon considering the head of X, and what happens to it under append. As X is the left-hand member of the append, its head must appear as the head of the final list – look at the example of the append above. This means that you can make the statement:

```
appending (X1 | X2) onto Y will give (X1 | Z)
```

In other words, the head of the appended version will be the same as the head of the left-hand list in the append, for some Z. Also, it should be clear that Z is simply the append of X2 onto Y. This gives a recursive condition, and the whole definition could be written as:

```
append(() Y Y)
append((X1 | X2) Y (X1 | Z)) if append(X2 Y Z)
```

This works as follows. The left-hand list in the append is split into head and tail, X1 and X2. The head forms part of the answer in that append, which is left pending until the rest of the routine comes to an end. The tail, X2, is then appended onto the right-hand list, Y, and this causes the recursive loop to be entered. This process repeats exactly as described before until the empty list is generated, when the recursion climbs back out, building up the final list as it goes. Note that this is tail recursive as the recursion is written in the final position in the definition, and the definition is both neat and economic on memory. Out of interest, note that the main work performed by this, or any other, recursive routine is not done during the repetitive recursion, but is all crammed into the final climb out of the recursion.

To appreciate the power of recursion, consider performing the same routine using conventional looping methods. This would require intermediate storage of variables, and a rather longer definition.

The following is an example of the relation's use:

```
all(X:append((A B C) (D E) X))
```

which gives the answer (A B C D E).

Append is also useful for adding a new head onto an existing list, and this way can be used to build up lists. For example, to add 'John' onto the head of the list:

```
(is walking)
```

we could write:

```
all(X:append((John) (is walking) X)
```

Note that the arguments of append are always lists, and thus the word 'John' must be placed within a list to be appended onto the other list.

The relation can also be used to check on an append, and the following is a true statement:

```
is(append((1 2 3) (2 3 4) (1 2 3 2 3 4)))
```

One of the most important applications for append is in its ability to be used in reverse, and hence to split up lists. For instance:

```
all(X:append((1 2 3) X (1 2 3 4 5 6)))
```

gives the right-hand list of a pair which when appended gives the long answer list in the append. The answer will thus be (4 5 6), which is the right-hand part of the list (1 2 3 4 5 6). The left-hand part can also be found, of course, in the same way.

This logic can go even further, because the definition of append is so simple, and contains no problematic relations. This means that more than one argument can be left unknown, which produces a most surprising result. Try the following:

```
all(X Y : append(X Y (1 2 3 4)))
```

This asks for a pair of lists which when appended together give the list (1 2 3 4). You should be able to see that there are several possible answers, but the set is finite, and not large. The answers given by micro-PROLOG will be:

```
() (1 2 3 4)
(1) (2 3 4)
(1 2) (3 4)
(1 2 3) (4)
(1 2 3 4) ()
```

This is an excellent way of generating all the possible splits of a list for use in other relations in list processing. Note, however, that this does not give all possible sublists of a list, it just gives the possible sublists which would append to give the main list.

This can be taken further by giving some pattern structure to X and Y above. For instance:

```
all((X1|X2) Y : append((X1|X2) Y (1 2 3)))
```

gives all the lists which append to give (1 2 3) such that the first of the two lists has at least one member. Remember that in the form (X1| X2), X1 is the single member at the head of the list, and X2 can be any type of list, including the empty list. The answers to the above are:

```
(1) (2 3)
(1 2) (3)
(1 2 3) ()
```

The append relation is so flexible that you can even leave all the arguments unknown! If you try the following, the answers are infinite, and you may have trouble stopping your machine without losing memory. If you are happy to try it, type in:

```
all(X Y Z:append(X Y Z))
```

The result should surprise you. All possible triples of lists such that the first two append to give the third will be the result, or at least as many as possible! To make the answers a little more manageable, you should use the 'one' keyword which was introduced some time ago, and has not been needed until now. Try:

```
one(X Y Z:append(X Y Z))
```

This will at least allow you to choose to stop the machine when you are tired of the process. The first few answers to this query are:

```
() X X
(X) Y (X|Y)
(X Y) Z (X Y|Z)
(X Y Z x) y (X Y Z x|y)
```

and so on. Note that the number of variables in existence soon runs out, even using integer subscripts, and after a little while question marks will probably appear in lieu of variable names. As you can see, micro-PROLOG uses the 'followed-by' symbol to define the structure of the general lists it is finding, but cannot, of course, give the variables actual values. However, this illustrates the remarkably flexible nature of the important append relation.

The structure of the arguments in the append relation can be defined in any way which fits in logically. For instance, you could specify that the right-hand list of the appended pair always starts with a specific value, or always has a specific value in its third place, and so on.

## append in AI

In terms of the analysis of sentence structure in natural language, this relation has some very powerful applications. For instance, suppose we construct a sub-language where just two verbs are allowed, and these are to be confined to simple sentences, and pairs of simple clauses without punctuation. We will choose the verbs:

```
jumps   runs
```

We will also forget about the correct inflexions (word endings) for different persons, tenses, etc., and stick to these spellings religiously. Even with these quite restrictive conditions, a surprisingly large number of possible ideas can be generated.

An example of a complete sentence composed of a pair of simple clauses would be:

```
John runs to the stile and jumps the stile
```

This sentence contains two basic clauses, and the append function can be used to separate them out. Assuming that we know who the subject of the clauses is throughout, the distinguishing feature of each clause is the verb. Thus, to analyse this sentence, we need two clauses which when appended give the complete sentence. Furthermore, we want the split to be at the verb, in order to separate out the two pieces of data contained in the sentence.

The following performs this:

```
all(X Y:Z EQ (John runs to the stile and jumps the stile)
          & append(X Y Z) & (either Y EQ (jumps|X1)
                                       or Y EQ (runs|X1)))
```

This will actually give two possible splits as follows:

```
(John)    (runs to the stile and jumps the stile)

(John runs to the stile and)   (jumps the stile)
```

These two splits start with the verb, and allow the next part of a routine to analyse the separate clauses as single statements one at a time. This relies to an extent upon the set structure of the sentences being used, though it is a step towards a general method of analysing complex sentences. One of the most direct applications of even these simple ideas is in the type of question and answer routines which are required by a computer system. It is usual to specify the form of the user's reply, and using the ideas above, more complex, and hence more life-like responses will be allowed. This is a step towards the more intelligent machine.

Another important relation for analysis of sentences, as well as lists in general is the relation which is used to tell whether a given object is a member of a list. This is described next.

## The contained-in relation

In the above example it would have been useful to ask whether one of the two allowed verbs was contained within the sentence. This would also be a first step towards finding which of a number of verbs is present, before causing the sentence to be split up, perhaps at each verb found, for analysis.

The contained-in relation has the following form:

```
X contained-in Y
```

where X is a member of the non-empty list Y.

The recursion, in the normal manner, considers the head and tail separately. If X is the head of Y, then the relation is true. Otherwise, if it is the head of the tail of Y, the relation is similarly true. Thus, there are two rules:

```
X contained-in (X|Y)
X contained-in (X1|X2) if X contained-in X2
```

Once again, this definition is tail recursive. Also, the 'simplicity' of this definition makes it very flexible. It can be used to check a 'contains-in' relationship between two items, or it can be used to generate members of a list, or even lists given a member. For example, the following uses the relation:

```
is(A contained-in (A B C))
```

and the answer is YES.

If the first argument is left unknown, the relation generates all members of the list in the second argument, separately. Thus:

```
all(X:X contained-in (1 2 3))
```

has answers:

```
1
2
3
```

This can be used, within another relation, to feed the members of a given list to the relation conditions one by one.

If the second argument is left unknown, then as for append, an infinite set of lists will work. Try:

```
one(X:A contained-in X)
```

and answer the question which comes up in the affirmative a few times. This will generate the following set of lists:

```
(A | X)
(X A | Y)
(X Y A | Z)
(X Y Z A | x)
and so on.
```

These are general lists which have A as a member, and examining them helps in understanding the way in which list structure works. The important thing to remember is that the tail, after the'|' symbol, can contain anything, while the head part is clearly defined. The first list shown is simply any list which has A at its head, including the singleton where X is empty. The next list characterises any list of two or more members with A as the second member, and so on. The lists simply place A at all the different positions possible in a general list, with unknown members.

If you want to be entertained, sort out the answer to:

```
all(X Y : X contained-in Y)
```

The append and contained-in relations form some of the most basic functions needed for processing lists. They are also useful in related areas such as general set theory, where all the standard rules and functions such as Union and Intersection, etc, can now be defined, but this is conveniently left as an exercise at this point!

As a simple example in sentence analysis, and continuing the example in the previous section, consider the following:

```
all(X is a verb in the sentence:X contained-in
        (On Mondays John jumps the river)
        & (either X EQ runs or X EQ jumps))
```

This looks for one of the two standard verbs in the sentence, and prints it as part of a message. The answer would be:

```
jumps is a verb in the sentence
```

This gives a few starting ideas in the analysis of lists of words, and the general trick is to consider a set of rules which are satisfied by the parts of the sentence to be found.

## Further examples in sentence structure

The type of analysis introduced above can be extended to finding the subject of the verb, as long as it appears immediately before the verb. Accordingly, we have to construct a logical statement containing rules which are only satisfied by the word preceding the verb. This will pick out the word required uniquely, and it can then be used in another part of a relation, or printed directly. No matter where the subject and verb combination appears in the sentence, we will assume that they are always next to each other with the subject first. This means that the sentence structure is of the form:

(A . . . B subject verb C . . . D)

where any number of members can appear before and after the subject-verb pair. Such a list can be constructed in general by appending any list onto another which has the verb in the second place. This is equivalent to:

```
append(X (Y verb | Z) sentence)
```

Thus, append can be used to find all such combinations in a given sentence. The value of Y, here, is the member which precedes the verb, and thus, by definition, the subject being sought. The verb can be runs or jumps, and this is catered for in the following:

```
all(X is the subject:(either Z EQ jumps or Z EQ runs)
    & append(X1 (X Z | X2) (Today and everyday John
             runs home to his parents)))
```

This matches sublists of the sentence list with the pattern having a verb in the second place, and when successful returns the word in the first place.

The criterion chosen here for deciding whether a word is a verb is very inefficient. In a later chapter we will use a unary relation to define verbs, and thus store all the allowed verbs on the database. We can then use a single relation to see whether a given word has the attribute of being a verb. This also allows the easy expansion of the number of allowed verbs.

The above is a highly inefficient way of inputting sentences for examination, and the next chapter will show how to allow general input from the keyboard to be examined.

*Example 4.3*
(1) Show how to use append to find sublists of people Mary likes which start with a male.

(2) Construct a binary relation called 'is-verb-in' which will pick out all the verbs in a sentence given that John is always the subject, and always appears just before the verb. Give an example of its use.

(3) Define a relation which gives all the lists of the likes database which contain at least one pair of males next to each other. For instance, the list (John Harry George) satisfies the condition more than adequately.

## Building up lists from others

Just as we can use recursion to build up numerical values, it is also possible to build up lists. The same principles hold as above, but instead of adding numbers together, as the recursion climbs back up the ladder, lists are built up member by member. Examples of this have already been seen in the last section, and we will now look at some examples which use these ideas to query our 'likes' database.

As an example, let us look at the program of Figure 4.1 which finds the males liked by Mary. By now it should be clear to you that the flowchart form used there is somewhat different from the actual process involved in a recursive routine. However, it is also true to say that there is a certain amount of transfer of ideas, and the basic process of head stripping, for instance, is common to both.

The main trick in constructing a recursion is to use the definition itself on the next lower list or number, in some sense. Thus, in several of the examples above, a relation being defined was used on the tail of the given list, and this caused a sequence of tails to be examined, ending at some point, and then climbing back up to give the answer.

To find the list of males liked by person X, we will define the relation:

```
X likes-male-list Y
```

where X likes a list, Y, of males. To make the problem easier, we will be content with more than one list of males if there are several lists which X likes containing males. Look at the database and you will see that Mary, for instance, likes two lists of people, and the answer will thus be two lists, each containing just the males from each such list. The main part of this relation involves picking out the male sublist within a list of people. To do this, we will define a new relation:

```
X male-sublist-of Y
```

where X is the list of males contained in Y. To define this relation recursively, consider the structure of Y as (X1 | X2). If the head, X1, is male, then append it to the male sublist of X2, otherwise simply return the male sublist of X2 alone. This is a recursive definition, and it strips the head off successively until the tail is empty. Thus, the final rule must deal with finding the male sublist of the empty list – this is clearly the empty list itself. The definition is thus:

```
() male-sublist-of ()
X male-sublist-of (X1 | X2) if Z male-sublist-of X2
          & (either X1 male & append((X1) Z X)
                or X EQ Z))
```

This is quite involved, but follows the above explanation. An important point to note is that append must have only lists as arguments, and hence the brackets around X1 in the first argument above. A single member cannot be appended onto a list, it must be contained in a singleton list to append correctly.

This relation has the defect that it tries to find all possible lists which satisfy the relation, and not just the maximal list. Thus, if the following is typed in:

```
all(X : X male-sublist-of (Paul Mary George Sue Harry))
```

the answer set starts with (Paul George Harry) and then goes on to all the sublists of this, including the empty list. This is due to the backtracking of micro-PROLOG, and though a judicious redefinition of the relation may alleviate this problem, there is a quicker and easier way which is explained in the next section.

## Stopping the backtracking using /

The backtracking function of micro-PROLOG is one of its most useful and powerful attributes, but as we see above it can also be pedantic. The '/' symbol can be used to switch it off. This symbol is simply placed in the conditions, as if it were a true statement, and all backtracking will cease at that point, even if there are actions still to be considered. This symbol is used with an '&' conjunction, but is ignored when reading the definition logically. It only has a control function – that of preventing further backtracking.

To prevent the backtracking above, it should be placed at the end of the conditions in the second rule for the male-sublist-of relation. The definition thus becomes:

```
() male-sublist-of ()
X male-sublist-of (X1 | X2) if Z male-sublist-of X2
          & (either X1 male & append((X1) Z X)
                or X EQ Z) & /)
```

The space before the '/' symbol is important to prevent its being mixed up with the '&' symbol. The example given in the last section now has a singular answer:

```
(Paul George Harry)
```

and no backtracking occurs to produce more than is needed.

We can now, finally, write out the complete program for the relation of Figure 4.1. It is as follows:

```
X likes-male-list Y if X likes Z & Y male-sublist-of Z
```

This definition starts by generating a list Z such that X likes Z, and the next part of the definition extracts just the male sublist from this Z. As explained above, there is no backtracking in the solution to finding the male sublist. However, the main definition above includes no '/' symbols, and it will backtrack to find all the candidates for Z on the database. This means that no answers for Y will be left out, but the unnecessary sublists of each answer will not be produced.

For the above definition to work, both append and male-sublist-of must be stored on the database. This gives an example of a complete non-trivial program where several relation definitions work together to achieve the end.

Try the following:

```
all(X:Mary likes-male-list X)
```

This has two solution lists. Now try adding in '/' to prevent the second from being given.

The slash does not need to be placed at the end of the relation. Wherever it is placed, the backtracking will go up to it and no further. Thus, if it is placed halfway along the conditions, all conditions after the slash will be backtracked over, but none of the previous conditions. This is illustrated in the answer to the following example.

*Example 4.4*

(1) In the query of Example 4.3 (1), there were two main backtracking procedures. Show where you would place '/' in order to limit the final answer to a single list. Show where you would place the slash to limit the answer to giving all the sublists of just the first value of Y.

(2) Rewrite the query definition of Example 4.3 (3) so that the lists given in answer appear just once, instead of more than once if there is more than one pair of males present.

## Summary

**Recursion** This is the process of allowing a definition to use itself. This causes an automatic iteration. The process is powerful enough to avoid the need for any of the normal looping keywords of other languages.

It is important to remember that a recursive definition, as any other iterative procedure, must have an exit definition, or the recursion proceeds for ever.

In micro-PROLOG, if the recursive part of a definition appears at the very end of that definition, it is called 'tail recursive', and the stack of pending operations will not continue to grow as it is executed.

**append** Although this is a user-defined relation, its importance is such that it will be used throughout the language. It is a ternary relation, and simply joins the lists given in its first two arguments into a larger list. This list value is then given to the third argument. It can also be used in reverse to split lists into parts.

/ This symbol prevents backtracking wherever it is placed in a definition. That is, backtracking will occur up to it, but no further.

## Solutions to problems

*Example 4.1*

(a) (i) The empty list is not all-male because it is not a singleton male list, and the recursion cannot match (X1 | X2) to it. If the first definition of the relation, including the empty list, had been used, the answer would have been YES.

(ii) NO is the answer because george does not start with a capital letter, and thus it is simply not recognised as being defined.

(iii) Paul is not all-male because it is not a list.

(b) This relation is almost identical to the all-male relation, except that instead of the heads being checked for the male relation, it is checked to see whether it 'likes' anyone. The logic is exactly the same as all-male, and its definition is as follows:

```
X sociable-list if X EQ (X1) & X1 likes Y
X sociable-list if X EQ (X1 | X2) & X1 likes Y
                    & X2 sociable-list
```

The following would be examples of using the relation:

```
is((Mary Sue) sociable-list)
```

This has the answer YES because each of the list's members likes at least one person.

The following gives all the sociable lists on the database:

```
all(X:Y likes X & X sociable-list)
```

The likes relation is used to generate all the lists on the database, and each one is examined to see whether it contains people who like others.

This gives the answer:

```
(Mary)
(Mary)
```

It is a typical feature of micro-PROLOG that too many answers are given in many common situations. If you have to avoid this for some reason, it is crucial that you understand why it occurs in any given definition. Here it occurs as follows:

The database is scanned for a list, X, which has members who like someone else. The first occurrence of such a list is (Mary), as you should be able to see by looking at the database. This is a singleton which contains someone who likes others – namely Mary. Thus the first rule for sociable-list succeeds, and X is printed. However, the backtracking action of micro-PROLOG then looks down the database for another occurrence where X likes someone else, before the complete backtrack occurs to find another X. Mary, of course, likes two lists, and this ensures that there are two successful checks on Mary, each of which causes a separate print of (Mary) before full backtracking occurs to find another list value for X.

If you are interested, you can check that this is the case by two manoeuvres. Firstly, delete the second rule for sociable-list, and try the above query again. This proves that it is the first rule which causes the double print. Then add another fact to the database which says that Mary likes some list or other – any will do – and the query will print (Mary) three times!

*Example 4.2*

(1) The lists involved can be generated by the 'likes' relation, and then passed onto the 'length' relation. This is done as follows:

```
all(X:Y likes Z & Z length X)
```

micro-PROLOG finds a Z which is liked by anyone, and its length is then found. Backtracking causes the other lists to be found, and each has its length calculated. If you have the database suggested above stored in the machine, the answers will be:

```
3, 4, 3, 1, 5, 5
```

(2) The general form of the relation is:

```
X not-likes-number Y
```

Its definition starts by generating all the lists on the database. Each one is then tested to see whether X likes it, and calculates its length if not. This is done as follows:

```
(X not-likes-number Y if X1 likes X2
             & not X likes X2  & X2 length Y)
```

Using this definition the following:

```
all(X:Mary not-likes-number X)
```

has the answers 4, 3, 1 and 5, as you should be able to see from the database.

(3) The factorial function is used as follows:

```
X factorial Y
```

where Y is the factorial of X. The definition is similar in structure to that of integer-sum. The recursive part of the definition uses the fact that factorial of X is equal to X times the factorial of X−1. The ending rule is the fact that 1 is factorial of 1 – i.e.:

```
1 factorial 1
```

It is important to exclude the case of the given number being negative, and this leads to the use of LESS as before, with all of its restrictions for reversibility. The definition is thus:

```
1 factorial 1
X factorial Y if 1 LESS X & SUM(Z 1 X)
              & Z factorial X1 & TIMES(X1 X Y)
```

Once again, this is not tail recursive, and will use up memory quite quickly. It is a good test of the available memory of different computers to compare how high the given number can be before memory runs out. Of course, the presence of the SIMPLE module affects the memory capacity available quite drastically.

The relation is used as follows:

```
all(X:5 factorial X)
```

which gives the answer 120, as you should expect.

*Example 4.3*

(1) The query depends upon finding a list which Mary likes, and splitting it into sublists, each of which has a male head. The backtracking finds all other such lists. The query is:

```
all((X1|X2) is such a sublist:Mary likes Y &
       append(X3 (X1|X2) Y) & X1 male)
```

This is not the only representation of this definition, and you might have used a single variable in place of (X1 | X2), for instance, and then matched the single variable with this pattern later. The only test of accuracy is to try the definition out, and see if it gives the same answer as above. With the standard database suggested at the start of this chapter, the answers should be:

```
(John Harry George)
(Harry George)
(George)
(George Sue Pam John Mary)
(John Mary)
```

There are two backtracking paths, one to find more Y values, and one to find more sublists of Y.

(2) We must find all the sublists starting with John, because we know that the second member will always be a verb. The relation will be used as follows:

```
X is-verb-in Y
```

where X is any verb in the sentence Y. The definition uses append to split the list Y into sublists which must have at least two members with John as the head. The second member, must be a verb and is the value of X. The full definition is:

```
(X is-verb-in Y if append(X1 (John X | X4) Y))
```

Again, you might have used a more long-winded definition where the append gives a sublist, then the sublist is matched to a pattern and finally checked for head John. This does not matter, but the above is the neatest form.

An example of the use of this relation could be:

```
all(X is a verb:X is-verb-in
      (Hello there when does John arrive))
```

This gives the answer:

```
arrive is a verb
```

The power of this technique cannot be over-emphasised. It allows a very sophisticated matching and analysis procedure to be implemented simply by writing down a couple of simple rules which the answers you are seeking satisfy.

(3) The relation required is a unary relation. It takes a list in one argument, generated from the database, and checks to see whether it contains a pair of males next to each other. We will call the relation 'mlist' used as follows:

```
X mlist
```

which returns an affirmative answer if X is such a list.

The point here is that the required list can contain a pair of males next to each other anywhere in the list, not just at the head, for instance. The general pattern for such a list would be a list X such that:

```
append(X4 (X1 X2 | X3) X) where X1 and X2 are male
```

This simply uses append to define a list X containing any list X4 (possibly empty) followed by a list with at least two male members next to each other. This does not restrict the answers to male pairs in any specific position within the answer list. The definition is:

```
(X mlist if append(X4 (X1 X2 | X3) X)  &
                            X1 male & X2 male)
```

This relation cannot be used to generate lists which appear on the database, it must be placed within a query which generates such lists for checking. The problem is solved by:

```
all(X : Y likes X & X mlist)
```

The answers to this will be:

```
(John Harry George)
(John Harry George)
(Pam John Harry George Mary)
(Pam John Harry George Mary)
```

The reason for the doubling is that in backtracking over the mlist relation in this query, micro-PROLOG finds that there are two cases where each of the two main answers fit the conditions. For instance, in the first pair above, it will match the pattern in mlist to the pairs John Harry and Harry George. We will see in a later example how to prevent this.

*Example 4.4*

(1) The query in Example 4.3 (1) just requires a slash to be added in the very last position to limit the entire query to a single answer. The query thus becomes:

```
all((X1|X2) is such a sublist:Mary likes Y &
            append(X3 (X1|X2) Y) & X1 male & /)
```

The execution will forward track along the conditions finding an answer, and at that point will meet the slash. The potential track back along the rules will thus be halted. To allow the backtracking over the last few conditions, but prevent it from finding any more Y values, the query must be written:

```
all((X1|X2) is such a sublist:Mary likes Y & / &
           append(X3 (X1|X2) Y) & X1 male)
```

This allows the backtracking only as far back as the slash, by which time it has found all the sublists of the first Y value. It goes no further.

(2) The query in Example 4.3 (3) causes micro-PROLOG to backtrack over the mlist relation as many times as necessary for each value of X found by the 'likes' relation. This can be stopped using '/'. However, it is no good placing the symbol at the end of the query itself, or no more values of X will be found either. The slash must be placed within the definition of mlist to prevent the repetition. To achieve this, simply place '& /' at the very end of the definition of mlist. This solves the problem.

# Chapter Five
# Some Extra Features, and Parsing

## Introduction

The aim so far has been to introduce micro-PROLOG's main features, and to illustrate the art of thinking in terms of logical programming. The programs we have seen have involved the use of a set of rules which the answers have to satisfy. micro-PROLOG works through the given database and solves the problem according to these given rules. It is not generally necessary to spell out the intricacies of that process to the interpreter. This is a rather different approach from that normally found in the BASIC-type languages.

In addition to this intelligent method of programming, micro-PROLOG has a number of features of an advanced nature such as full floating point numbers, and tail recursion. However, in some ways we have only just scratched the surface of the language. To appreciate the full complexity of micro-PROLOG, you should work through the literature which comes with the language, and try out all the examples.

The normal implementation of the language also comes with a number of extra modules which can be loaded in for a variety of uses. We have used one of these exclusively so far, namely SIMPLE. There are others including a different front end processor, a special program for loading and constructing new modules, a numerical package, and so on. We will use one of these extra modules called 'TOLD' when we look at input of data via the keyboard. However, we will not look here at the other modules available, and you are well advised to read the manual which comes with the language to find out how these are used.

In this chapter we will look at some of the inherent facilities which have not been mentioned before, and then move to an example of a longer micro-PROLOG program. The program will be constructed to perform a limited but useful form of sentence analysis, called *parsing*.

We will continue to work in SIMPLE, and you are advised to do what you can to maximise the memory available to the programming, on your machine.

We will start by looking at a couple of extra keywords which have not been introduced before. This is still within the SIMPLE front end processor, and it must be loaded if you are using a computer. The 'likes' database of the last chapter will also be needed, in these first sections, to illustrate the ideas presented.

### The isall keyword

The 'isall' condition is used to produce a list from the set of all answers to a query. For instance, in the query:

```
all(X : Y likes (X|Z))
```

the answer would be all the heads of the lists on the 'likes' database. These answers would simply be available one at a time, and not bound together into a single entity such as a list. isall is used to bind all the answers into a single list. Its general use is as follows:

```
X isall (Y:some conditions)
```

X is the list of all the answers, Y, for the conditions shown. For instance, the last example could be written as:

```
all(Z : Z isall (X : Y likes (X|X1)))
```

micro-PROLOG interprets this as meaning that all the answers to the query following isall, i.e. all the X's, are to be combined into a single list, and stored in Z. There is a further condition on Z which you should check on your particular implementation. The members of Z may be stored in the opposite order to the order in which the answers are found. Each new answer to the query can be thought of as being appended onto the front of the list, which starts off empty. However, it is best to check that this is so on your machine. Thus, the answer to the above, with the standard 'likes' database should be:

```
(Pam George Mary George George John)
```

This is the list of heads of all the lists on the database.

isall can be combined with other conditions to find more complex answers. For instance, it can be used to determine how many females a particular person likes. The following example uses the 'length' and 'contained-in' relations defined in the last chapter:

```
all(X:Y isall (Z:Mary likes X1 &
          Z contained-in X1 & Z female) &
               Y length X)
```

This finds all the females, Z, which are members of lists Mary likes, places them all in one large list Y, and then finds its length. The answer, as you can see from the database, is 3. You should now change this query to look for the number of males which one of the people on the database likes, and try to work through the logic to see how it works. This will help you to construct your own relations and queries.

Another important condition on the use of isall concerns the difference between its 'local' variables, and its 'global' variables. The local variables, to any relation, are those variables which only appear within the relation, and the global ones are those which also appear outside the relation. In the case of the last example above, only local variables appear, and they are, essentially, X, Y, Z and X1.

The condition is that any global variables which may be used must be defined before the isall condition is used. This is similar to many of the other relations we have met so far, and a generating function must appear before isall for these variables. An example of such a case can be given by rewriting the above query for the number of females liked by Mary. The new definition below will not give the same answer, in general, but it does illustrate the point:

```
all(X:Mary likes X1 & Y isall (Z:Z contained-in X1
          & Z female) & Y length X)
```

In this case, X1 is global to the isall relation, and it is important that it has a value when the isall is met. The value is given, of course, by the 'likes' generating function which simply hands lists which Mary likes to the rest of the query with each pass of the execution. Because there are two such lists to be examined by the isall, there will be two answers this time – one for each list. The answers given are 0 and 3, as you should expect from looking at the database.

As you can see, isall is used to produce list values which contain all the members subject to a given set of conditions in one go. This saves dealing with the individual answers to a set of conditions one by one. The isall relation is particularly useful for dealing with the theory of sets in mathematics, as is the next keyword.

## The (forall . . . then . . . ) condition

This allows a condition to be checked subject to another condition on a set within the database, without specifically constructing the set involved. For instance, we might wish to find all the females on the database who like just males. This would normally be done by generating females, along with lists they like, and then checking every member of every one of those lists to find which ones contain just males. To do this checking for males, it would be worth defining a new unary relation called male-list which gives an affirmative answer when applied to an all male list. Its definition, using recursion, would be:

```
() male-list
(X|Y) male-list if X male & Y male-list
```

This simply checks that the head is male, and if it is, applies male-list to the tail. The recursion ends when the tail becomes empty.

This would then be used to solve the previous problem as follows:

```
all(X:X female & X likes Y & Y male-list)
```

This will generate possible females, find the lists they like and check each until one is found which is all-male. The female liking that list is an answer to the problem. The forall condition, however, can express this query in a different way. Its general form is:

```
(forall condition then condition)
```

The two conditions are general single or multiple conditions, possibly containing all the usual conjunctions. forall says that for all the values of the local variables satisfying the first condition, the second condition must hold. The brackets are essential, as they were for (either. . . or. . . ). In addition, the same local and global variable condition holds as it does for isall, and indeed for 'not', which was introduced in a previous chapter. An example of forall would be:

```
(forall X male & X likes Y then Y length 3)
```

This will give an affirmative answer if for every male X, X likes just 3 people. In other words, forall finds all possible variables satisfying its first condition, and then checks that each of them satisfies its second condition. Any single failure in the second condition gives forall a negative answer immediately, without continuing the check. The forall condition above would fail on this database, because it is not true that every male likes just 3 people. You can confirm this by trying:

```
is((forall X male & X likes Y then Y length 3))
```

which will give NO as the answer. Note the double brackets. One set is the normal set for the 'is', and the second set is for the forall. This query can be changed to give a YES answer simply by changing the last condition such that it checks that the length of the lists found are less than 10, say. In other words forall, then checks to see whether every list liked by a male is less than 10 in length. This is clearly true, and the following gives the answer YES:

```
is((forall X male & X likes Y & Y length Z
                then Z LESS 10))
```

The solution to the problem of finding all the females who like just males could be written as:

```
all(X:X female & X likes Y & (forall Z contained-in Y
                     then Z male))
```

This generates a possible female value and a list she likes to be handed on to the forall for checking. Admittedly it still uses an external function, contained-in, as did the last method of solving this problem. However, this is a useful general function, and no special functions need to be constructed for this query.

It is easy to produce apparently reasonable sounding logic, in these complex conditions, which is actually quite fallacious. For instance, in the last example it might have been tempting to try the following form:

```
all(X:X female & (forall X likes Y & Z contained-in Y
                       then Z male))
```

Here, female X's are still generated, and each is handed on to the forall for checking. It might appear that this simply involves finding Y lists which she likes, and checking to see whether it is an all-male list. If so, the forall is affirmative, and Y is an answer. However, this is not the complete story. The error comes with the fact that forall means exactly what it says – for every possible value produced by the first condition, the second must hold. The first condition here produces all the possible Y lists which the female likes, including, inevitably, ones which are not all male. The forall then founders and returns a negative answer.

As a general rule, it is worth trying to put all the generating functions before the forall, and placing the minimum number within the forall, consistent with the effect. Remember that each condition placed within the forall may be a potential generator of a single wrong value which will make the entire forall fail.

## Memory space

The next section deals with the important activity of allowing the user of the program to input values from the keyboard as the program is running. However, this may well require you to load in a new module, depending upon how your particular system is configured, and this will use up memory. As a consequence, it may be useful for you to be able to tell how much memory there is left to play with. This is done in SIMPLE by using the SPACE relation, which is used as follows:

```
all(X:X SPACE)
```

If you wish to see how much memory is available before loading SIMPLE, then you will have to type the command in a somewhat different form. For the moment, simply accept it and it will become clear when we look at the standard syntax in the next chapter.

```
?((SPACE X)(PP X))
```

This must be copied verbatim - except that any variable can be used in place of X.

The result of either of these commands will be to print the number of K bytes left for programming. If you try this before and after loading SIMPLE, you will see why your programs are likely to overflow while using SIMPLE on a very small machine.

## The is-told keyword

In general you will find that you need to load a new module to use this command, and the normal form of this loading is something like:

```
load TOLD
```

if you are in SIMPLE, or

```
LOAD TOLD
```

otherwise.

This will not use up a large amount of memory compared to SIMPLE, but if you are using a very small machine, the loss in memory will be significant. You should keep an eye on the amount of memory available to you by using the SPACE relation shown above as you proceed. For instance, you may have trouble containing the likes database, with all the functions we have defined for it, in memory all at once, as well as loading and using TOLD.

The following gives some simple examples of the use of is-told which just uses the basic database of likes, male and female facts. You can delete the other relations and facts if you wish.

The general form of the is-told condition is as follows:

```
(message X message) is-told
```

where X is a variable. In fact, any number of variables can be used, intermingled with messages, and micro-PROLOG will expect you to input your values in the correct order, as with INPUT in BASIC.

Note the brackets containing the complete list of variables and messages. As with the INPUT word in BASIC, it is possible to have messages printed along with a request for the value of X from the keyboard. The command above would normally be included within a query or definition, and when micro-PROLOG reaches it, a request is made, via the screen, for a value to be placed in X. As a simple example of the use of is-told, try typing in the following:

```
all(X:X is-told)
```

This uses a single variable, with no messages, and as such will normally not require brackets to contain the variable. It simply asks for a value from the keyboard to give to X, and then prints it as an answer to the 'all' command. The screen should show something like:

```
X ? .
```

and it is waiting for a specific form of response, which consists of one of four possible words. If you simply type in a value instead, it will be ignored, and you will be asked to input the correct form of response. To see this, type in the number 34 at this point. The machine should tell you that only one of the following is allowed:

```
yes    no    ans . . .    just . . .
```

The answers 'yes' and 'no' are used to allow you to input true and false as responses to relational questions. For instance, you might include the condition:

```
(X male) is told
```

in your program, in which case the machine asks you to input whether X is male or not using 'yes' and 'no'. However, in the numerical example above, you should reply with 'ans' or 'just', followed by the value which you wish to give to X. The first of these, ans, will allow the process to repeat, and asks for another value when the first has been used. The second response, just, finishes after the current input has been used. Thus, to see the above working repetitively, you will have to use 'ans'. The following is a typical set of responses:

```
X ? ans 34
34
X ? ans 67
67
X ? just 5
5
No (more) answers
&.
```

The 'all' performs the task of printing the final answer to the query each time, which here is simply the value of X which has been input.

As an example of including messages, type in the following:

```
all(X:(input X please) is-told)
```

This gives:

```
input X please ?
```

and your responses are printed as before. To include messages in the answers printed too, simply include the message as normal in the 'all' command. For instance:

```
all(value is X:(input X please) is-told)
```

This gives the same response as above, and when you type in:

```
ans 34
```

for instance, the machine replies with:

```
value is 45
input X please ? .
```

This gives some reasonable flexibility in making the interaction as meaningful as possible.

The more usual situation with the use of is-told is that the value input is used in later conditions to produce an answer. For instance, to construct a routine which gives the lists of people liked by someone, we could allow the user to input the person's name. The query would be written:

```
all(Y likes list X: (input person Y) is-told &
                      Y likes X)
```

As usual, each part of the routine passes values onto the next as micro-PROLOG forward tracks, and then backtracking keeps the routine looking for other solutions. A typical interaction would be:

```
input person X ? ans Mary
Mary likes list (John Harry George)
Mary likes list (George Sue Pam John Mary)
input person ? ans Harry
input person ? .
```

The only words typed by the user are 'ans' followed by Mary and then Harry. The rest is produced by the machine. Notice that when no answer exists, the machine simply repeats its request for a value. Where more than one answer exists, all are printed separately as shown.

is-told allows you to input different values for the lists to be examined, instead of having to include them in the query, or rely on the data in the database. For instance, in our examples of sentence analysis, we generally included the whole sentence within the query each time. The next section uses keyboard input for the examples it examines.

## Further sentence analysis and parsing

We will now look a little further into the analysis of standardised sentences, inputting them from the keyboard. Sentences will be allowed to be of arbitrary length, but restricted to being composed of clauses each of which is separated from the previous one by a specified conjunction, 'And'. This particular spelling is chosen as a quick way of preventing any confusion with the reserved word 'and'. We will further restrict the clauses to being simple subject, verb, object types, with no indirect objects. We will allow nouns to be preceded by the word 'the', in-lower case only, if necessary. These rules allow sentences of the form:

John repairs cars
Sue reads the book
Dogs like biscuits And they chew sticks And Pam likes dogs

Note that there are no subjects left understood, and that all the verbs are 'transitive' - that is they take direct objects. Each verb is given a subject and an object. These severe restrictions on the form of the sentences allow us to start the business of building up programs without undue complexity. The conditions can then be relaxed, bit by bit, to allow quite complex communications to be made.

The analysis we are going to perform will simply pick out the subjects, objects and verbs in the types of clauses and sentences shown. This is an aspect of an activity called 'parsing', which literally means splitting into parts. This is considered to be the first step towards the intelligent management of natural language sentences. The 'intelligence' is knowing what to do with the parts once they have been extracted from a given sentence.

The answer to this is not yet fully understood, but part of the answer is to tie the words themselves up with a dictionary to find out the meaning. Other parts of the process will be bound up with using the position of the given words within the sentence. For instance, in our first example above, as John is the subject, cars is the object and repairs is the verb, even if we knew nothing about any of these words, we would at least know their relationship. That is, something called 'John' does something called 'repairs' to something called 'cars'. This is a powerful piece of information, vague though it may appear.

In order to relate our sentence words to other words in the sentence, we are relying above on position. This is highly restrictive, but necessary, at least at first.

The study of sentence structure is generally made easier in languages where 'inflexions', or endings to the words, are used to signify their relationship to other words, and to define other useful information about the words. For instance, 'he repairs' and 'he repaired' differ only in the tense of the verb. This is signified by a change of inflexion which is definite and unique. To tell whether the sentence is set in the present or the past, we simply look at the end of the verb 'repair'.

Unfortunately, in English, these inflexions are largely missing, and it is not in general possible to relate one word to another by inflexion alone. Other languages do allow this type of analysis. One of the best languages for such an analysis is Latin where the inflexions obey remarkably rigid laws, in most cases, and it is usually possible to jumble a sentence around, and still pick out its meaning. Try the same with English sentences, and the meaning will change radically. For instance, consider:

John repairs the car

and

the car repairs John.

In a fully inflected language, these two sentences would mean the same thing, as they would in any other order, because that relationship would be locked up in the inflexions. That is, the fact that John is the subject would be able to be seen from the word ending, and this would have to change in order to make John the object.

In summary, there are two prime avenues to explore as a result of the parsing: one is to understand the meaning of the words themselves, and the other is to understand their relationships within the sentence.

As explained above, we will save any problems with the relationships within the sentence by sticking to a rigid format.

The first example is to extract the subject, verb and object of each clause within a sentence typed in through the keyboard. We will begin by examining sentences which have just one clause containing subject, verb and object, in that order. This will form the basis for solving the more general problems above. Thus, we will look at sentences of the form:

(the) noun verb (the) noun

which possibly have the definite article before either or both of the single-word nouns.

If the definite articles were known to be missing, the resulting simple form could be parsed just be matching it up with (X Y Z), and printing the fact that X is the subject, Y is the verb and Z is the object. However, the problem here is that the list can vary in length from three to five members, and when conjunctions are allowed, the list can be even longer. We need a method of analysing the words sequentially to parse the sentence.

One method of dealing with the sentence would be to start by removing all the definite articles, and thus produce a more predictable form for analysis. However, a true parse of the sentence should include the definite, and eventually the indefinite, articles. The parsing method used below will be naturally expandable.

The final object of the parsing will be a list of the words with a description of each to show that the parsing has been successful. For instance, the result of parsing the following sentence:

the cat jumps the wall

should be a parsed sentence list similar to:

(the definite-article
cat subject
jumps verb

the definite-article
wall object)

Note that a capital letter is not used for 'the' at the start of the sentence to make the matching easier.

The method we shall adopt will be to look at the head of the sentence and see whether it is the definite article. If so, it is identified as such, and the next member is found, and is the subject. The next word will be the verb. The word after the verb is again compared with 'the', and either identified as such, or is the object. We will write this as a separate relation called 'clparse-to' because this will be of use in parsing the clauses in the larger sentences. It will be used as follows:

X clparse-to Y

where X is a single clause sentence and Y is the parsed sentence, with each member identified.

The logic for the program is shown in Figure 5.1. It depends heavily upon the standardised nature of the clause structure involved, and produces a list containing all the words of the sentence followed by a standard identifying label. If any given sentence can be analysed into standard clauses, then this program will complete the parsing.

Figure 5.1 works as follows. The clause to be parsed is matched up with (X| Y), and the head is thus matched with the variable X. This is checked to see if it is the definite article. If it is, the variable x is set equal to a message list which says that 'the' is present in the given clause, and that it is the definite article. This is the start of the final parsed list. The rest of the clause is then matched up with (y z| X1). This is to extract the next two words which must be a subject and a verb. If 'the' was not found, however, the list x is set to the empty list, and the whole of the initial list then matched up with (y z| X1). The reasoning behind the program so far is to ensure that y contains the subject, with 'the' stripped off if necessary, and z contains the verb. Also, the list x is the start of the final parsing, with or without 'the' as the first word parsed.

The next step is to record the fact that the subject and verb have been found, in y and z respectively, by storing them in Y1 along with the previous value of x, plus the appropriate messages. Thus, at this point, Y1 is a partially parsed list containing everything up to and including the verb.

The remainder of the clause is held in X1, if you look back, and this will inevitably be a list – either two words including 'the' and the object, or a singleton containing just the object. This is catered for next in a similar way to the treatment of the subject. X1 is split into Z1 and x1, and Z1 examined to see if it equals 'the'. If so, then x1 will be a singleton list, whose head is the object. This head is then extracted by matching x1 up with (y1| z1), and thus y1 equals the object. The final parsed list is then constructed by appending 'the' and the object, with labels, onto Y1.

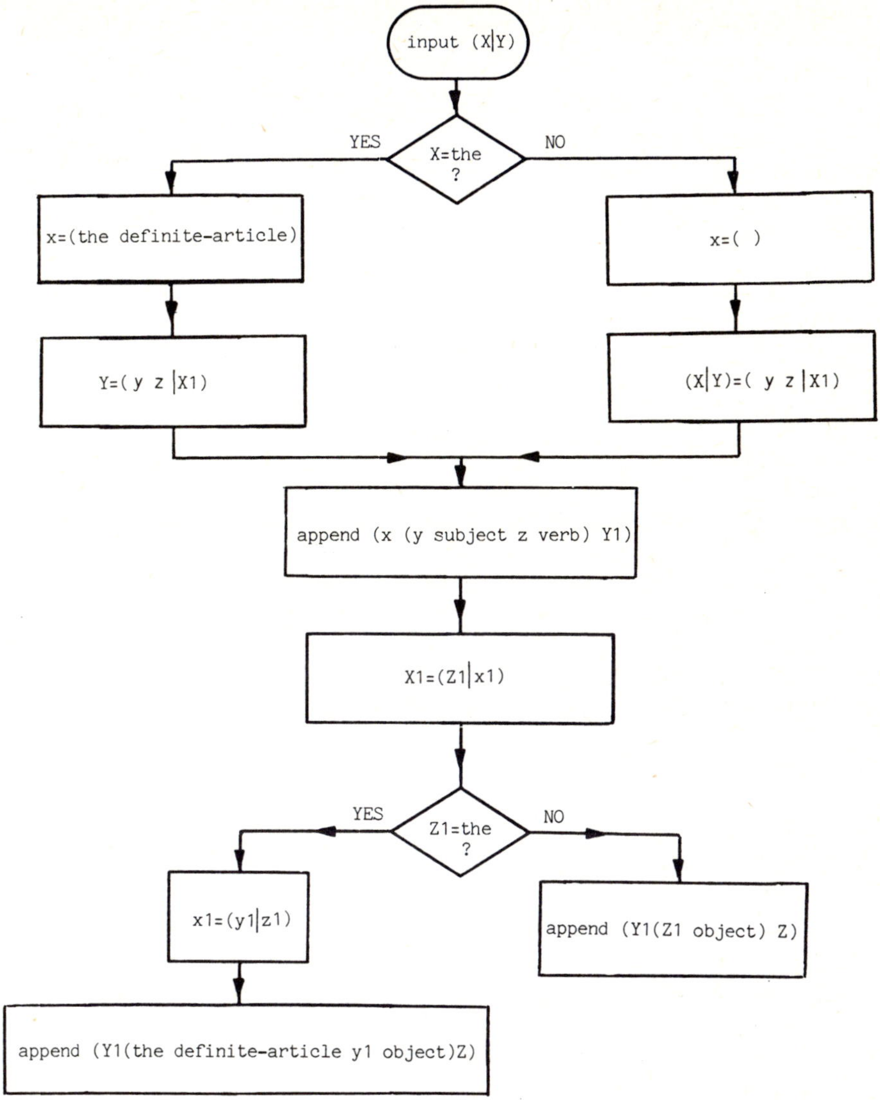


*Figure 5.1.* Flowchart for clparse-to.

If Z1 was not 'the', then it must be the object itself, and this can simply be appended straight onto Y1, with a label, to form Z.

This procedure is not very general, but it serves well enough for the purposes of analysing parts of our standardised sentences. We will see shortly how to use it to parse sentences containing an arbitrary number of standard clauses.

The flowchart of Figure 5.1 is sufficiently near to micro-PROLOG to be able to code almost directly into rules for 'clparse-to'. It is important to realise that a diamond-shaped decision box in Figure 5.1 will translate into an (either . . .or . . .) form when coded. You should have a try at coding as much as possible for yourself before reading on.

The following is the full program, which can be typed in and tried:

```
((X | Y) clparse-to Z if

   (either X EQ the & x EQ (the definite-article)
                                   & Y EQ (y z | X1)
    or   x EQ () & (X | Y) EQ (y z | X1))

   & append(x (y subject z verb) Y1)
   & X1 EQ (Z1 | x1) &

   (either Z1 EQ the & x1 EQ (y1 | z1)
         & append(Y1 (the definite-article y1 object) Z)
    or   append(Y1 (X2 object) Z))

   & /)
```

Note that this program will require the definition of 'append' to be present. The last rule in the program is '/' to prevent backtracking once the single required answer has been returned. Check through the program for yourself and see if you can tell what will happen if backtracking is allowed. Then try removing '/' and see if you were correct.

To use the program, it is well worth loading TOLD, and using is-told, or you will end up with far too much typing to do. To test a program in general, you should try to apply every type of example which can occur. In many cases this is an impossibly difficult task. Here there are only four possible types of data. Clauses can contain three words, four words with a 'the' in one of two places, or five words, with two definite articles. You should try all these types of data in the program.

An example of the use of the program is as follows:

```
all(X:Y is-told & Y clparse-to X)
X ? ans (cat jumps wall)
(cat subject jumps verb wall object)
X ? ans (cat jumps the wall)
(cat subject jumps verb the definite-article wall object)
X ? .
```

This tries out two of the possible clause types. As you can see, the answer is simply a repeat of the clause, word for word, with each word followed by a single-word description. This allows another program to search through the parsing, and pick out the object, for instance, without having to perform the analysis each time. This would be done by searching the parsed list for a pair of members with the word 'object' in the second place.

A next step might be to pass this to another program which is trying to 'understand' who is the subject of each input clause, and working out 'who is doing what' by looking at the verb. Another program, of a more specific nature, may be looking for activities which a particular person is performing. Whether the person being sought is the subject or object of a verb is thus crucial.

You should practise using this program a few times, and check that you fully understand the form of the answers being given, before proceeding.

The next program inputs a longer sentence, composed of simple clauses, and produces a complete parsed list. It is done by splitting the sentence into sections separated by 'And', as mentioned above. A neat way to do this is to define a recursive relation which starts by stripping the first clause off the given sentence, and handing it to clparse-to. It then works on the rest of the sentence in the same way. We will call this relation 'parse-to', and it completes the simple parsing in this example. It is used in exactly the same way as clparse-to.

As with any recursive relation, the first rule must cater for the ending of the routine. In this case, the clause stripping will end with a simple clause being parsed, eventually, when all the previous clauses have been dealt with. However, to deal with this simple clause, it must first be recognised as such. This can be done in a number of ways, but we will use the 'contained-in' relation of the last chapter, to check whether it contains the word 'And'. It is most important that you do not try to use 'and' in the sentence, because it is a reserved word, and will cause an error. The use of an upper-case A for the first letter will save any problems. Also, make sure that the definitions for 'contained-in' and 'append' are both present for the following. However, to limit the amount of memory used, nothing else is needed on the database.

Thus, the first rule of 'parse-to' will be:

```
(X parse-to Y if not And contained-in X
               & X clparse-to Y)
```

This ensures that only simple clauses are parsed using clparse-to. You can try 'parse-to' exactly as for clparse-to, but this time try adding in the word 'And' anywhere in the sentence to see that this prevents the parsing from being performed.

The next step is to construct the general recursion. This is best understood by considering a typical sentence to be parsed such as:

```
the cat jumps the wall And John follows the cat
               And Harry follows John
```

Remember, 'The' is not allowed, and 'And' is the spelling of the conjunction. The routine will start by extracting the first five words, and parsing them as a simple clause. The 'And' is used to determine the end of the first clause, and the start of the next. With the first clause stripped off, 'parse-to' can begin to work on the rest of the sentence in exactly the same way. A possible definition could be:

```
(X parse-to Y if append(X1 (And | X2) X)
     & X1 clparse-to Z & X2 parse-to X3
     & append(Z X3 Y))
```

When this definition is encountered, it is certain that there is at least one 'And' in the list X, or it would have been dealt with by the first definition for parse-to. Thus, when the first append is met, it is able to split the given value of the sentence, X, into two pieces. The first, X1, is a simple clause as the append will work from left to right in X, until it encounters the first 'And'. At that point, X1 and X2 are given values, and the 'And' is effectively stripped off.

The next step is to parse X1, and allow parse-to to act on X2. The results of these two parsings are appended together and stored in Y, which is the final answer.

This routine picks out the simple clauses correctly, and acts upon them using clparse-to. However, the result will be a single list, as before, but with the result of parsing several clauses, and it is not so easy to see where one parsed clause ends, and the next begins. From the list processing point of view, it would be useful if instead of simply discarding the 'And' conjunctions, they were still preserved as separators between clauses, in some way. The best way to do this would be to keep the separate clauses in separate sublists within the fully parsed result. This preserves the structure of the original sentence, in terms of clauses, and keeps the parsings separate. It will also be necessary to prevent the backtracking from producing other irrelevant answers to the problem.

The above changes can be achieved by a very small adjustment. In the final append where the final list is constructed, brackets should be placed around Z and X3. This forces the parsings of each clause to be held within separate lists. The backtracking can be prevented using '& /' as the very last rule in the definition.

This produces the complete parsing program which will work with sentences composed of as many clauses as you like, joined with 'And'.

The full program is:

```
(X parse-to Y if not And contained-in X
              & X clparse-to Y)

(X parse-to Y if append(X1 (And | X2) X)
      & X1 clparse-to Z & X2 parse-to X3
      & append((Z) (X3) Y) & /)
```

To use the program from the keyboard, type in:

```
all(X:(input sentence Y) is-told & Y parse-to X)
```

An example of an interaction would be:

```
input sentence X ? ans (the cat jumps the wall
And John leaves the house)
((the  definite-article  cat subject jumps  verb
the definite-article  wall  object) (John subject
leaves  verb the definite-article house object))
```

As you can see, the parsed result is not easy to read quickly, but it is now in a thoroughly machine-accessible form. The answer itself only has two members, each being a sublist. Each sublist is composed of pairs of words, the first of which is a given sentence word, and the second is a one-word description of its relation to the other words in the sentence.

Using the products of this program will be easy, and a useful exercise would be to write a program which accepts this output, and prints out such things as the number of clauses contained in a sentence, or a list of the verbs used, and so on.

To increase the scope of the sentences allowed, you should now add in the ability to detect other conjunctions such as 'Then' and 'Or', (again, note the spelling). Another refinement would be to allow the indefinite article, with both spellings: 'a' and 'an' to be used before nouns, and also a first capital letter to the articles, so that they could be used at the start of a sentence with capitals.

This method of parsing illustrates how larger programs are built up in micro-PROLOG using intermediate definitions such as 'append' and 'clparse-to' to achieve the result. This naturally brings a type of modularity to the programs which helps to make them easy to read and alter, and generally well-structured. The program also practises recursion in a general application, as well as list analysis.

As to parsing, this program is not particularly general as a parser, as it relies heavily on a rigid sentence structure. One way around this is to use a dictionary to recognise verbs and nouns, and then assume that the subject appears before the verb, and the object after. This is more general in terms of the rigidity of the sentence form, but is more restricted in terms of memory, and the actual words which are available for use. Another type of problem occurs with the very large number of words which double as verbs and nouns. Parsing always comes down to either insisting on some rigidity of form, or making contextual sense of the words used. For instance, we can make sense of the following sentence with a minimum of thought:

```
robot wall jumps
```

However, to a parser, the following two sentences would be equally valid restatements of it:

```
robot jumps wall
```

and

```
wall jumps robot
```

The context is obviously important, and we are appealing to an almost unimaginably complex plethora of experience, locked up within our brains, when we decide that the first sentence is the correct restatement. After all, how many robots have you actually seen jumping anywhere? Also, it may be possible for a wall to jump over a robot if the wall is small enough, and is pushed hard enough, but we just 'know' that this is rubbish! To give a machine this type of understanding is not easy.

## Summary

**isall** This is used to combine the answers to a routine into a single answer list. Its use is as follows:

```
Z isall(X: conditions)
```

This causes Z to collect together all the X's which satisfy the conditions shown. All global variables must be defined, and Z may have the answers in reverse order. You should check this.
**(forall . . . then . . .)** The conditions before 'then' are used to generate variable values for the conditions after 'then'. If all the values passed to the conditions after 'then' cause these conditions to be satisfied, the forall will succeed. If one condition is broken, the process ceases and the forall fails.
**is-told** This relies on a module called TOLD having been loaded, on many machines. It allows keyboard input to programs, and has the form:

```
(messages and variables) is-told
```

This causes the machine to print the messages, and ask for values for the variables, in order, to be typed in. The response must begin with one of four words. 'yes' or 'no' can be input if a true or false value is appropriate to the question. If 'ans' is typed in, this can be followed by values for the variables, and the routine will repeat. If 'just' is typed in, followed by a set of values, the routine uses the values, and then ends.
**SPACE** This command allows the remaining memory space to determined. Its use is as follows:

```
all(X:X SPACE)
```

if using SIMPLE, and:

```
?((SPACE X)(PP X))
```

if not. The number which is printed is in K bytes.
**parsing** This means splitting a sentence into its components, and identifying the parts of speech, and their relations to the rest of the sentence.

## Chapter Six

# Standard Syntax, Further Natural Language Analysis, and Metalogical Programming

### Introduction

The subjects of this chapter are wide-ranging and complex enough to fill an entire book. They take us into the realm of the more complex uses of the language. micro-PROLOG, up until now, has been used almost entirely via the 'front-end' processor called SIMPLE. This is, effectively, an extra compiler which allows the user to employ high level programming commands which are then compiled into true micro-PROLOG commands. The micro-PROLOG commands referred to are couched in a language called the 'standard syntax'. The basic rules are similar to those of SIMPLE, but there are fewer keywords, and high level facilities. Standard syntax executes faster, and uses less memory. It is still a high level language, in the usual meaning of the word, but is considerably more efficient than SIMPLE.

We will use some standard syntax programming to define another method of analysis in the important AI area of natural language comprehension. This area is at the basis of much of the current research into intelligent machines, and the fifth generation computer systems are based around PROLOG, and as such should be well adapted to its study.

Metalogical programming is a technique which allows the values of variables to include relations and complete programs. By this means those relations and programs can be manipulated by other relations and programs. This gives the ability to produce some very complex structures, which we will only just introduce in this book. Once the main ideas of logical programming, and their application to AI are established, you will find that this new avenue provides even greater flexibility to a language which is already sophisticated, by any standards.

### An example of a standard syntax program

Even though we will not use SIMPLE in these sections to write programs, it is instructive to load SIMPLE at this point, and type in or load one of the relations you defined above. By this means you can observe the compiler at work, converting your SIMPLE definition into standard syntax. Assuming that append is present, if you type in

```
list append
```

the familiar response should be

```
append(() X X)
append((X|Y) Z (X|x)) if
    append(Y Z x)
```

Now try typing in:

```
LIST append
```

The response this time, which you should notice is faster, will be in standard syntax:

```
((append () X X))
((append (X|Y) Z (X|x))
     (append Y Z x))
```

There is not such a large difference, except that the 'if' is missing. This word does not exist in standard syntax, it is simply assumed by the position of the lists within the definition. The other difference is the fact that there are quite a few double brackets. This is largely due to the fact that the append function is no longer written in prefix form, but is written at the head of a list which contains the arguments in its tail. This is the only form which relations may take in standard syntax, including all unary and binary relations.

If you are interested to see a large program in standard syntax before proceeding, try:

```
LIST clparse-to
```

assuming that the definition is still stored on the database, or that you have reloaded it. All the main parts of the program are present, but the form is different. You will note that EQ is still present in standard syntax, which is the reason for its being written in uppercase throughout. The same is true of programs using LESS, and so on. Note that the EQ again appears at the head of a list with its arguments in the tail.

To proceed further, you should start the machine from scratch, and thus ensure that there are no modules present. We will not need SIMPLE, and it is better to free the memory space for programming. Also, the commands of standard syntax are written in upper-case throughout, and you can set your CAPS LOCK key on if you have one. You can still use lower-case for variable values; it is only the standard micro-PROLOG keywords which are in upper-case.

### Rules of standard syntax

The commands and keywords of standard syntax are simpler than those of SIMPLE, but rather less readable. However, the increase in speed and memory efficiency make standard syntax essential in serious programming.

The SIMPLE sentences and relations are converted into 'clauses' and 'atoms', and the connectives 'if' and 'and' are not available. All standard syntax programs can be analysed into atoms and clauses. An atom is anything which previously used a relation name – for instance, the relations male, female, likes, EQ, contained-in, etc. These were written in prefix, infix or postfix form, with a relation name and a set of arguments. In standard syntax, these forms do not exist; they are all converted into the same form, with the relation name at the head of a list, with the arguments, in order, in the tail. There are no variations to this, which should make the situation easier to remember.

For instance:

```
Harry male              becomes    (male Harry)
X EQ Y                  becomes    (EQ X Y)
Mary contained-in X     becomes    (contained-in Mary X)
```

Notice how the order and general form of the arguments remain constant, it is just the way in which the relations and facts are written which has changed.

The above relations are all expressed, therefore, as lists, which are called atoms.

Programs and relations stored on the database can only ever be in the form of 'clauses', which are simply lists of atoms. The atoms above cannot in their present form be stored on the database without being converted into clauses. For instance, we can no longer store a fact such as:

```
(male Harry)
```

on the database. It is essential to place it in a clause. This can be done simply by writing an extra pair of brackets around it, and thus converting it into a singleton clause, containing just one atom:

```
((male Harry))
```

This can be stored on the database by typing it in directly – you do not have to use any equivalent of the 'add' command. You will soon become used to double pairs of brackets in standard syntax, and most of the initial errors you make will probably be due to too few brackets.

When you type in the above clause, the micro-PROLOG supervisor program recognises its form as a clause, and adds it to the database. To see this, try typing just the atom, with a single set of brackets, and then try the clause with two sets of brackets. The first should give an error; the second will be accepted, which you can only tell by the fact that the &. prompt appears instead of the '?' symbol. In general you will discover, too, that the &

prompt is a reply which signifies the same as YES in SIMPLE, and the question mark signifies NO.

Now try typing in:

```
LIST ALL
```

and you will see that this is equivalent to the same command in SIMPLE, but with upper-case letters. The clause you have added to the database should be printed out as the sole member of the database, unless you typed it in more than once.

LIST is used in the same way as for the SIMPLE 'list'. For instance:

```
LIST male
```

will list all the members of the male relation on the database.

The word KILL also acts just as for the SIMPLE form, and it can be used to KILL ALL or to KILL male only, for instance. We shall meet some of the other database manipulation functions shortly.

The next point is to be able to store rules containing more than one atom, equivalent to the SIMPLE 'if' statements. Remember that any such definition had just one 'if' in it, and always separating the first relation from the rest of the sentences in the definition. This is still true of the standard syntax, except that as the 'if' always appears at exactly the same point each time, namely after the first atom, it can be omitted. For instance, the following:

```
X likes Y if X likes Z and Z likes Y
```

contains three relations, each of which converts into an atom of the form:

```
(likes X Y)
```

and the 'if', as usual, occurs after the first of them. This converts to:

```
((likes X Y)(likes X Z)(likes Z Y))
```

The supervisor accepts this clause typed exactly as above, and, as with every clause it receives, simply assumes the 'if' between the first two atoms, and the 'and' between the subsequent ones, no matter how many there might be. This economy of words can make the standard syntax hard to assimilate, not just because words are missing, but, as you will see, the exact position of the brackets in a complex expression decides where the 'ifs' and 'ands' are to be assumed.

In order to formalise the situation, the relation name, at the head of a list containing arguments, is called the 'predicate symbol'.

The formalism introduced above has the great advantage of economy of word usage, as well as clarity and accuracy. It is not as easy to read, but there is little reliance on English words, with their confusingly complex shades of connotation and meaning. The mathematical clarity of the standard syntax gives it a certain elegance which many languages lack in their attempts to bring the exactness of the computer to a level which uses a redundancy of English words almost for the sake of it.

A standard syntax program is simply a number of rules stored on a database, each of which contains just clauses of atoms.

## Some previous relations in standard syntax

We will now practise the above by rewriting some useful relations into standard syntax – for instance, the immensely useful append relation. To save having to swop between upper- and lower-case letters on the computer, we will define everything in upper-case, though lower-case will work just as well.

The append relation, would be added to a SIMPLE database using:

```
add(append(() X X))
add(append((X1|X2) Y (X1|Z)) if append(X2 Y Z))
```

In standard syntax, add is not needed, and the relations are written within clauses, in atomic form, with APPEND as the predicate symbol as follows:

```
((APPEND () X X))
((APPEND (X1|X2) Y (X1|Z))(APPEND X2 Y Z))
```

Again, the supervisor recognises the first of these as a singleton list, being a clause containing a single atom, and simply adds it to the database verbatim. The second clause contains two atoms, and you will have to examine the brackets very carefully to sort out its two members. When this is executed, the micro-PROLOG supervisor program effectively inserts an 'if' between them. If a third, and subsequent atoms had been written into the clause, they would all, effectively, have been preceded by 'and'. Note that upper-case has been used for APPEND purely to keep the typing easy – lower-case would do just as well.

Another example is the length relation which used to be stored on the database as:

```
(() length 0)
((X|Y) length Z if Y length x & SUM(x 1 Z))
```

The standard syntax form of the first one is almost immediate, as it is simply a singleton fact, or atom. A little rearrangement and an extra set of brackets to convert into a list, or clause, is all that is needed. The second is equivalent to a clause of three atoms. Again, the 'if' always appears at the start, and this standardised position makes it redundant. Similarly, 'and' always appears between the second and subsequent atoms, and is also omitted in the standard form. The standard syntax form, which can be typed in directly, is

```
((LENGTH () 0))
((LENGTH (X|Y) Z)(LENGTH Y x)(SUM x 1 Z))
```

Here, again, the general rule is to change all existing rules, such as SUM, to atomic form. Once again, remember that there is an automatic 'if' implied between first and second atoms, and an automatic 'and' between second and third.

A good exercise is now to return to some of the longer programs in this book, change them into standard syntax, and see if the new versions agree with the compiled forms stored on the database for those functions. The only problem is reading them back with micro-PROLOG's changes of variable name – it can make the checking rather difficult.

### More complex conditions in standard syntax

All the other SIMPLE conditions such as 'not', 'forall', etc., have straightforward equivalents in standard syntax, and you simply have to learn their new forms as described below.

The (either . . . or . . .) condition acts on two clauses, one before the 'or' and one after. In standard syntax, these two clauses are arguments of the OR predicate symbol. For instance:

```
(either X likes Y & X male or Y likes Z & Z female)
```

becomes:

```
(OR ((likes X Y)(male X))((likes Y Z)(female Z)))
```

You must examine this structure carefully, because the exact position of the brackets determines where the '&s' are. This is a relation having two clauses as arguments. The first clause has two atoms, anded together, as does the second. There are no 'ifs' in this structure because the whole condition is just a single atom, having OR at its head, as the predicate symbol. It is very important to remember that the arguments of OR have to be clauses and not atoms.

The negative, 'not', has two possible forms depending upon whether a single relation is negated, or the relation negated is larger and contained within brackets.

The simpler type:

```
not Mary male
```

becomes

```
(NOT male Mary)
```

while the more complex form:

```
not (X likes Y)
```

becomes

```
(NOT ? ((likes X Y)))
```

which can also be written:

```
(NOT likes X Y)
```

because only a single relation is being negated. However, the following:

```
not (X likes Y & Y likes Z & Z female)
```

becomes:

```
(NOT ? ((likes X Y)(likes Y Z)(female Z)))
```

Note that in the forms where the negated condition is a list, there is a question mark following the NOT. Note also that the negated list is placed within a clause, and not an atom, following the '?'.

isall and forall are a little more complex to translate, and you will have to stick carefully to the following forms.

The isall relation used to have the form:

```
(X isall (X1 X2 X3 : X1 female & X1 likes X2
                     & X2 likes X3))
```

This simply produced the complete list of answers to this query. The following is the standard syntax form:

```
(ISALL X (X1 X2 X3)((female X1)(likes X1 X2)(likes X2 X3))
```

The ISALL predicate symbol takes three arguments. The first is the name of the final list of answers, and the second is the list of variables satisfying the conditions of the third argument, which is a single clause. The three atoms on that clause are all automatically 'anded' together.

forall, like 'either or', takes two arguments corresponding to the first and second set of conditions. Thus:

```
(forall X male & Y female then X likes Y and Y likes X)
```

would become:

```
(FORALL ((male X)(female Y)) ((likes X Y)(likes Y X)))
```

Each argument is a clause, and the atoms are 'anded' together within the clauses.

## Adding and deleting on the data base

ADDCL and DELCL are used to add clauses and delete clauses on the database respectively. They can both be used as direct commands when followed by single clauses. For instance, the following would add a new clause to the database:

```
& ADDCL ((female Mary))
```

As you can see, the ADDCL command can be typed in directly after the system prompt, just as LIST can, for instance.

The delete command can be used in a similar manner:

```
& DELCL ((female Mary))
```

Both of these commands also have a two-argument form. This form is used to enter a number representing the position in the database where the addition or deletion is to take place. However, in this two-argument form, they cannot be used as commands, only as parts of a relation definition or program. ADDCL and DELCL in this form are meant to be included within programs to manipulate the database in a general manner. The use of ADDCL is as follows:

```
(ADDCL X Y)
```

where X is the added clause, and Y is the position after which the clause is to be added. In other words, the clause in the position Y is left there, and X placed after that clause with everything else shifted down. This is different from the SIMPLE command 'add' where the added clause was placed in the position given in the numerical argument.

DELCL is used in a similar manner:

```
(DELCL X Y)
```

where X is the clause to be deleted, and Y its actual position.

## Reading and writing and comments

There are some primitive printing and reading relations, which were not needed in SIMPLE, though they can be used there perfectly well. They are P, PP and R.

The printing functions, P and PP, give two basic forms of printout, and are used to head a list of any number of items to be printed within an atom. Thus the following:

```
(P Hello X there)
```

can be used within a definition to cause 'Hello' to be printed followed by X, or its value if it has one, and then 'there'. These are printed in a sequence with spaces as separators, and the cursor ends up immediately after the word 'there' ready for the next printing command. Note that the above is not a direct command to be typed in and executed, it is merely an atom in a larger construction. To position the cursor on the next line following this printout, in order to give separate lines to subsequent outputs, use:

```
(PP Hello X there)
```

The SIMPLE forms of these relations is:

```
P(Hello X there)   and   PP(Hello X there)
```

In fact, we have used PP before. When we wanted to know the amount of space available to us, we simply type in:

```
?((SPACE X)(PP X))
```

The reason for the '?' will be given in the next section, but by now it should be clear that it is followed by a single clause, with two atoms. The '?' tells micro-PROLOG not to place an effective 'if' between the first two atoms, but simply to 'and' all the atoms in the clause together. The effect is to give X a value equal to the number of K bytes left for program memory. This value is then passed onto the PP atom, which is always true, and as a by-product is designed to print its arguments, or their values.

Using PP above gives interactions of the form:

```
& ?((SPACE X)(PP X))
15
&.
```

where 15 is the value of X. If P were used instead, the interaction would look like this:

```
& ?((SPACE X)(P X))
15&.
```

The cursor is left in the position immediately following the printout, rather than being stepped to the next line.

The other relation introduced above, R, gives a method of inputing data from the keyboard, and is less 'fussy' than is-told, which requires you to type in various words along with the data. When you use R as a predicate symbol, the arguments following are set equal to the values you type in, in order, and the routine simply prompts you with '.' until the variable values are satisfied. There are no special words to type in, and the condition does not auto-repeat. To see an example of this, try typing in the following, again using the '?' which is explained in the next section:

```
?((R X)(PP X))
```

When this executes, the first clause allows the value of X to be typed in from the keyboard, and the second clause prints the value, returning the cursor to the next line as shown below:

```
& ?((R X)(PP X))
hello
hello
&.
```

The first 'hello' was typed in by the user, and the second printed by the computer in response.

The P, PP and R relations can be used in SIMPLE if required to produce a print or input at some stage in a routine. The relations are then used in the prefix form to print or input values of the following variables. This can have the advantage of allowing intermediate parts of a routine to be printed during the forward or backtracking, perhaps to help in analysing the process for debugging.

In SIMPLE, micro-PROLOG programs are usually fairly well self-documenting, but even then the need for comments within the program can arise. There is a special symbol '/*' for a relation which is always true, and whose arguments are disregarded by micro-PROLOG. For instance, the following allows a comment to be typed in which will not be evaluated:

```
(/* This is a comment)
```

In SIMPLE, the form is:

```
/*(This is a comment)
```

There are more complex uses of comments available, but you should check your particular manual as these are dependent on implementation.

## The query '?' primitive

There is only one type of query in standard syntax, and we have seen its form above. It uses the '?' which you can think of as analogous to 'is' in SIMPLE.

A '?' at the start of a clause tells micro-PROLOG that the following is not to be placed on the database, and hence is not a definition containing an 'if' followed by conditions. Instead, it takes the atoms of the given clause to be 'anded' together. micro-PROLOG then performs a normal forward and backtracking execution of the atoms, effectively trying to solve them, just as in a SIMPLE 'all' or 'is' statement. If this requires values to be found from the database, or calculated, this is done exactly as before, and then handed on to the next atom for its use. As before, all the familiar rules about generating functions hold whereby some relations need values for their variables before being executed.

To use this query to its fullest extent, we really need some data and programs stored on the database. If you have stored your examples from the previous chapters of the book onto disk, or cassette, you could now load one of them in. You do not need SIMPLE to be present, because the data saved is always in the standard syntax form. It is only under SIMPLE that these data are converted into SIMPLE form for listing under the 'list' function. Thus, if you have a database called 'likes1' or something similar you could use the following to call it up:

```
LOAD likes1
```

This can be used later for you to practise using standard syntax.

However, we will start by loading a new database, and writing a new program to be stored on the database. This will give an example of a complete standard syntax session. However, you should bear the above suggestion in mind because it is a little easier to load facts onto the database using SIMPLE, and then revert to standard syntax to use them.

The next section gives an example of a different approach to the AI application of parsing sentences.

### A parsing program using standard syntax

The principle behind this example will be to store some facts about particular words on the database, and then use these to determine which words are nouns and which verbs, rather than relying on the exact position within the sentence. The aim will be to produce a similar output to the last example of a parser.

This time, the structure of the sentences allowed will be more general, but the parser will stick to producing just subjects, verbs and objects. Also, only those nouns and verbs stored on the database will be allowed.

To start the example, we will store some basic data on the database using upper-case throughout for ease of typing. It will do no harm to clear the computer completely, and start from scratch before proceeding. Type in the following data:

```
((NOUN JOHN))
((NOUN MARY))
((NOUN CAT))
((NOUN WALL))
((NOUN ROAD))
((VERB JUMPS))
((VERB LIKES))
((VERB WALKS))
```

This will do for a start, and you can extend it as you wish later.

The rules for the types of sentence allowed are, first, that no subject or object of a verb can be other than one of the nouns stored on the database, and the same is true for the verbs. Second, subjects must always precede the verb, and objects follow it. Other words can be interposed between nouns and verbs, but they must not include the given nouns above, as this will confuse our simple parser. Clauses are to be separated by AND, though this can be extended later, if you wish. It is not necessary to have a subject and/or an object for a verb, but if they are present they will be parsed. The parser will, again, split the output into sublists within the answer, one for each clause in the given sentence. Each sublist, however, will contain just subject, verb and object.

The general structure of the program will be the same as before, and we will begin at the top level, and define the parsing relation as PARSE-TO, which is used as follows:

```
?((R X)(PARSE-TO X Y)(PP Y))
```

This will simply wait for an input from the keyboard, and when you type in a sentence list it is given to X as a value, and passed on to PARSE-TO which parses it producing a value in Y which is then printed. The process does not repeat. If you wish it to, then one method is to define PARSE-TO to contain a (preferably tail) recursive loop which simply executes the above continuously until 'END', or something similar is typed in. Another method is to use PARSE-TO within another recursive definition which just performs the repeat. For instance, a new relation called REPARSE could be defined as follows:

```
((REPARSE)(R X)(OR ((EQ X END)(PP BYE BYE))
           ((PARSE-TO X Y)(PP Y)(REPARSE))))
```

This is tail recursive, which has the same basic rules as were introduced in SIMPLE. The relation being defined has no arguments. Its defining conditions are those following, and there is an implied 'if' after the first atom. If you count brackets and look closely, you should be able to see that there are two atoms following the implied 'if'. The second of these is split into two conditions 'ored' together. The first is true if you type in END, and the whole routine finishes there without tracking forward to the other OR condition. If the first is false, because a sentence has been input, then the parse is performed on the value of X input, and the answer in Y is printed. The recursion then causes the whole process to repeat. The first condition in the OR atom is the 'ending' condition for the recursion.

PARSE-TO is defined on similar principles to 'parse-to' in the last chapter. That is, the sentence is parsed clause by clause by a relation called CLPARSE-TO. In order to do this, we will need the relations for append and contained-in as before, but as you will probably have to type them in again anyway, we will keep their names consistent with the above, and define them as APPEND and CONTAINED-IN. The definition of APPEND is given at the start of this chapter, and you should type it in. Note that the definition of APPEND may not be accepted if SIMPLE is present. The translation of the other relation is straightforward, and very similar to that of append. You should be able to perform the translation for yourself, before reading on. To confirm your definition, it is as follows:

```
((CONTAINED-IN X (X|Y))

((CONTAINED-IN X (Y|Z))
     (CONTAINED-IN X Z))
```

which can be typed in directly.

To translate the SIMPLE relation parse-to into PARSE-TO you will have to use NOT, as explained in a previous section. In the SIMPLE version of the parser, it was also necessary to use '/', where it was added in the form '&/'. In standard syntax, & does not exist, and relations are simply placed in brackets, and including within the conditions after the implied 'if'. Thus the standard syntax form is simply (/). However, it turns out not to be necessary in the definitions below.

You should try to perform the translation of the SIMPLE form of the parser to PARSE-TO for yourself before continuing.

The complete translation is as follows:

```
((PARSE-TO X Y)(NOT CONTAINED-IN AND X)
     (CLPARSE-TO X Y))

((PARSE-TO X Y)(APPEND Z (AND|x) X)
     (CLPARSE-TO Z y)(PARSE-TO x z)
     (APPEND (y) (z) Y))
```

This generally follows the previous definition, and can be compared by loading in the SIMPLE version, and then using LIST. Note that NOT is used in its simplest form whereby it is negating a single relation. Under these circumstances it simply takes the relation to be negated as its second argument, and the relation's arguments as its own subsequent arguments as shown. The only problem might arise in your particular implementation if NOT is only available if SIMPLE is present – you will have to experiment with your machine to find out.

The next step is to define the required version of CLPARSE-TO, which will differ from the last version by the fact that the database is used to recognise nouns and verbs. CLPARSE-TO only has simple sentences to deal with again, but this time there are up to two nouns and a verb buried within an arbitrary number of other words. For simplicity, there will only be a maximum of two nouns and a verb in each clause, as defined by the database, and these will appear within the clause in the correct order for identification as subject and object. However, there may be only one noun, or none at all.

The basic idea will still be to strip the head off the clause, and OR relations will be used, as before, to ensure the correct decisions are made. Figure 6.1 gives a flowchart for the process adopted. The routine is recursive, but not tail recursive. It can be written in a number of ways which differ in detail, but the routine shown is consistent, and will be coded into standard syntax shortly.

As with all recursive definitions, there are two basic rules. The first (labelled (a)) simply says that the empty set parses into itself. This is used to end the recursion when complete.

The next part of the routine (labelled (b)) starts by matching the given clause to (X| Y) to extract the head. The final parsing is to be returned as the value of Z. If X is a NOUN, a check is done to see whether the rest of the clause, Y, contains a VERB. If it does, then X must be the SUBJECT, because it comes before the verb. If a VERB does not appear in Y, then this simple routine assumes that the VERB must already have been stripped off the clause, and the NOUN, X, must be the OBJECT. If X is not a NOUN, it

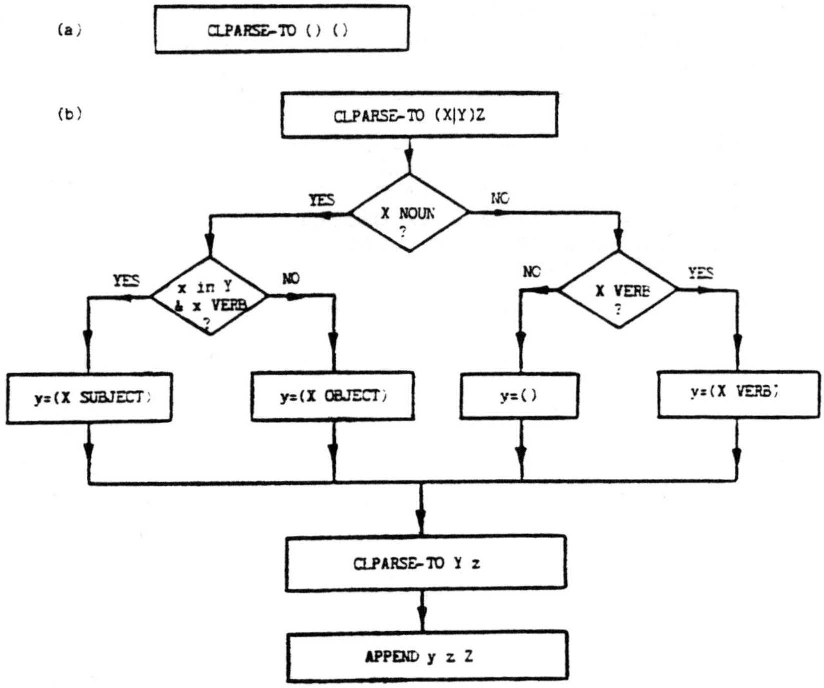


*Figure 6.1.* Flowchart for CLPARSE-TO.

is checked to see whether it is VERB. If neither of these, then this value of X is disregarded, and the process moves on to parse Y.

If one of the above checks is positive, that value of X is stored in the variable y, along with an appropriate parsing message. If the word is not recognised, then y is set to the empty list. At this point, y is the latest result of the parsing, and has to have the parsing of Y APPENDed on to it. This is achieved by parsing Y, and using APPEND as shown.

Recursion causes this routine to accumulate the APPENDs for later, and achieves the end as it climbs up the final ladder to the answer.

This provides a method of parsing clauses with a variety of forms. Clauses with just a verb and an object, plus any other unrecognisable words, will come out correctly – as will clauses with a subject and a verb, but no object. Even clauses with just a verb, and other words will be viewed correctly. The only problems arise when there is no verb present, or there are multiple NOUNs before and/or after the verb. Even then, a valiant attempt is made, and the result only slightly askew. This program gives a good example of a parser, and can be extended to allow quite complex statements to be analysed.

The coding of this routine is not difficult, but involves some nesting of OR statements. However, if you concentrate, and remember that the two statements in an OR must be clauses, and not just atoms, you will have little trouble. The final program is as follows:

```
((CLPARSE-TO () () )

((CLPARSE-TO (X | Y) Z)
 (OR ((NOUN X) (OR ((CONTAINED-IN x Y)(VERB x)
                     (EQ y (X SUBJECT)))
                    ((EQ y (X OBJECT)))))
     ((OR ((VERB X)(EQ y (X VERB)))
          ((EQ y ())))))
 (CLPARSE-TO Y z)
 (APPEND y z Z))
```

This has been arranged to show the various levels of nesting which are contained in the program. You should type it in as a continuous line, rather than trying to preserve the tabbing above. The computer will probably remove them anyway.

Now try some simple clauses, as follows, to see the power of this simple routine:

```
?((CLPARSE-TO (HELLO I SEE THE CAT JUMPS OVER THE
STRAIGHT WALL EASILY) X)(PP X))
```

Do not forget the '?' or the above will simply be added to the database, and will cause trouble later on.This is a very common mistake, and strange accumulations on the database normally arise from omissions of '?'. If you have input the NOUNs and VERBs suggested above, the result of the above will be:

```
(CAT SUBJECT JUMPS VERB WALL OBJECT)
```

Now try leaving out subject, object and then both. Then experiment with multiple nouns and verbs, and try omitting the verb entirely.

The complete program can now be tested by examples such as the following:

```
    ?((PARSE-TO  (TODAY  JOHN  WALKS  THE  STRAIGHT  ROAD
THOUGHTFULLY  AND  THE STRAY CAT JUMPS THE HIGH  WALL  AND
MEANWHILE MARY WALKS AWAY) X)(PP X))
```

This is a little long-winded, but shows how complex a sentence can be, even when composed of simple clauses, separated by AND, and containing NOUNs and VERBs as specified above. The solution to this is:

```
((JOHN SUBJECT WALKS VERB ROAD OBJECT)
(CAT SUBJECT JUMPS VERB WALL OBJECT)
(MARY SUBJECT WALKS VERB))
```

However, this will probably not be the form of the final printed output. The output will probably appear in a continuous form, from line to line. You should have a go at changing the program to output the answer in the above form.

This program will even sort out a reasonable parsing of such constructions as:

```
(JOHN LIKES AND JUMPS THE WALL)
```

This gives:

```
((JOHN SUBJECT LIKES VERB) (JUMPS VERB WALL OBJECT))
```

You can now use REPARSE to experiment with the program by parsing sentences which you input through the keyboard. As you use REPARSE, you will see that the input and output messages could do with being made more comprehensive. For instance, it would be useful to have an initial message such as 'INPUT YOUR SENTENCE NOW PLEASE'. Also, some extra lines between inputs and outputs will make the screen look better. This is achieved by the following version of REPARSE:

```
((REPARSE)(PP INPUT YOUR SENTENCE NOW PLEASE)
 (PP)(R X)(PP)(PARSE-TO X Y)(PP Y)(PP)(REPARSE))
```

This uses PP with and without an argument to print messages, and insert extra lines respectively. Even with the very simple printing facilities of P and PP, there is no reason why the program cannot be 'user friendly'.

## Extensions to the parsing program

The main extension to the above would be to extend the database of allowable verbs and nouns. However, there is a practical limit, of course. Extensions to the words parsed could include tests for conjunctions such as THEN, OR, and so on. However, the sentences given to the parser will still have to be written carefully.

Other parts of speech can be included, and an obvious extension is to allow adverbs ending in LY to be recognised, and associated with a given verb. The next step would be to allow the database to include examples of adverbs, adjectives, and so on. The problem soon becomes quite difficult, for the reason given before that many words have multiple usages. Also, complications arise such as the fact that adverbs, for instance, are allowed to qualify parts of speech other than verbs. It is important to remember that parsing is not simply a question of identifying parts of speech: their relation to the rest of the words in the sentence is crucial.

The analysis of sentences is at the heart of machine intelligence for the simple reason that any intelligent ideas which a machine might have must be transmitted to a human. This is done at present in a largely unintelligent manner, using formalised outputs, similar to the ones seen in the examples in this book. The next step is to give our machines a semblance of intelligence by allowing them to understand our natural languages. It is an interesting question whether it is possible to make a machine intelligent in our sense of the word, and there are those who believe it to be impossible. In many ways, the present level of intelligence with which we seek to endow our machines is only an apparent intelligence, based upon the use of words they cannot understand. Perhaps AI should be re-termed 'Apparent Intelligence'. However, the applications of AI, in any form, to industry and general computer use are manifold, and the starting point, in many ways, is speech recognition, and the use of natural language.

If you are interested in the further analysis of language, you would be well advised to buy a book on grammar. There are many good and readable works available from most good bookshops. One which can be recommended is the 'Teach Yourself Book' on English Grammar by B.A.Phythian. This book is comprehensive, and has plenty of examples to help in understanding the subject. As you read a book on grammar you will see that there is a certain mechanical logic to the way in which natural language is put together. Of course, there are also many complexities which can only be resolved by using very large data banks, and an intelligent expert systems approach to its use.

The aim of the PROLOG derivatives is to allow a user to store a set of rules, perhaps grammatical rules, on a database, and then write general queries which can be solved by using those rules. The problem is that many of those rules appear to elude us. If such could be found, the problem would be solved. The same is true, in fact, of general pattern recognition which is at the basis of many of the human faculties from the senses of sight and sound, to our sophisticated sense of touch.

Again, if a set of rules for speech or vision could be discovered, speech recognition and computer vision would follow immediately. It is an interesting question to contemplate upon whether such a position is actually theoretically possible. However, even this question remains unresolved at present.

## Metalogical programming

This subject has been left until last in this book as it takes us rather beyond our scope. The use of programs which manipulate other programs is complex but very powerful. We will not explore this avenue very far, but this gives an introduction to the field.

Metalogical programming is the manipulation of relations, rather than just alphanumeric constants, and lists. We have met some metalogical relations already. For instance, the SIMPLE relation 'defined' took a name as its argument, and gave a true answer if the given name was the name of a relation.

A useful operation which metalogical programming can achieve is the 'mapping' of a relation onto a list of sets of possible arguments of that relation. For instance, suppose some process produces pairs of numbers such as:

```
Y  =  ((2 3) (4 56) (3 4) (6 -3.1))
```

and we want to multiply each pair to produce a third. This can be done by stripping the head off the list, converting the list into separate members, acting the TIMES relation on them, and then dealing with the tail. However, it would be useful to have a general method of performing this 'mapping' of the TIMES function onto Y. We may, for instance, also need the two numbers added, and then divided and so on. A mapping function would act as follows, in the standard syntax:

```
(MAP X Y Z)
```

X is a variable having a relation name as its value, Y contains the list of argument lists for X, and the final result will be placed in the list Z. In SIMPLE, the form would be:

```
MAP(X Y Z)
```

The problem is to force TIMES, which is stored in X, to act on the members of Y. In SIMPLE this is achieved by using the 'true-of' relation which is available.

This relation is used as follows:

```
X true-of Y
```

where X is a relation and Y is a single list of arguments including the results of the relation. For instance, the following is a true statement:

```
TIMES true-of (3 4 12)
```

because 3 times 4 is 12. The order of members of the argument list must correspond to the normal order of the relation's arguments. The true-of relation cannot be used to generate a relation name, and its first argument must always have a value by the time true-of is executed. However, given this relation value, the arguments can be generated for it, if this is possible using the database. It should be clear that it is rather unfair to expect micro-PROLOG to generate all the answers to:

```
all(X: TIMES true-of X)
```

However, the following will work:

```
all(X: NOUN true-of X)
```

which should give:

```
(JOHN)
(MARY)
(CAT)
(WALL)
(ROAD)
```

We can use the true-of relation to map a ternary relation such as TIMES into a set of lists of arguments as follows, using SIMPLE:

```
(MAP(X () ()))

(MAP(X (X1|X2) (X3|X4)) if append(X1 (X3) Z)
                          & X true-of Z
                          & MAP(X X2 X4))
```

To understand this, as with most metalogical definitions, it is essential to be able to grasp which list level the various members of the lists are on. For instance, in the second rule above, the list (X1 | X2) consists of sublists, each of which contains, for instance, pairs of numbers for TIMES, stored in X, to act upon. The list (X3 | X4), on the other hand, is one level above this in that its members will not be sublists, but ordinary numbers resulting from the action of TIMES on the number pairs. This is not general, in fact, because instead of TIMES, the MAP relation may find itself applying to a ternary relation between lists, in which case the second argument of MAP will contain pairs of lists instead of numbers, and the third argument will just be answers, which again may be lists, to the relation X.

The point is that the heads of these lists, which are X1 and X3 are on different levels in terms of lists. This means that when the append is applied in order to form three-argument lists for X to act upon, it is necessary to bring X3 'down one level', to append onto X1. For instance, with TIMES, X3 will be a number, and X1 a list of two numbers – hence the brackets around X3 in the append.

The recursion above starts by acting X on a list containing the heads X1 and X3. These are appended to form a single list, with all members at the same level, and as for the TIMES example above, true-of can then act on the list to produce an X3 within the final list Z. The recursion then acts upon the rest of each list. The true-of relation is thus used here as a generating function for the answers to X acting upon the given sublist pairs.

Similar relations to MAP can be defined for binary relations, and many other more general mapping relations can be constructed. The above gives a reasonably simple but useful example of a metalogical approach to programming. There is considerably more to this subject, and the more advanced books on PROLOG will normally help you to explore this important area. It has been included here as a 'taster' to an important extension of micro-PROLOG which is a good next step for your study of the language.

## Conclusion

The material presented so far has been aimed at allowing you to pick up the essence of the language, along with a little insight into its applications. micro-PROLOG is more complex than many of the high level languages which you will encounter elsewhere.

The standard syntax has a number of other facilities, which you should discover by reading the manual with your version of the language. Some of the facilities which are available are dependent on dialect. The final chapter discusses some further AI applications using PROLOG.

## Summary

**Standard syntax** This is the underlying code in which micro-PROLOG programs are stored. SIMPLE can be used as an easy way to generate such programs, as its storage is always in standard syntax.
**Relation names** A relation name is called a predicate symbol, and appears at the head of a list, with its arguments in the tail. No other form exists in standard syntax for a relation.
**Atoms and clauses** An atom is a list containing a predicate symbol at its head, and a set of arguments for that relation in its tail. A clause is a list of atoms.
**Adding to the database** A clause typed directly into the machine will be added onto the database. An implied 'if' is placed between the first and second atoms, and 'and' between the second and all subsequent atoms. By this means, the first atom is defined 'if' the subsequent atoms are all true.
**Queries** A clause precede by '?' will be executed rather than added to the database. It is assumed that all the atoms of the clause are 'anded' together.
**LIST and KILL** These commands are used in the same way as their lower-case equivalents in SIMPLE.
**ADDCL and DELCL** These commands are followed by a clause, and will add or delete this clause to and from the database. They both have versions which allow the position of the clause to be defined, but this facility can only be used within a program.
**NOT** NOT can be used as a predicate symbol in an atom, and its arguments are either a single relation name followed by its arguments, or '?' followed by a single clause containing the atoms to be negated. The atoms in this clause are all assumed to be 'anded' together.
**OR** OR is used as a predicate symbol, as is NOT, but always has a pair of clauses as its two arguments. The two clauses are the OR conditions.
**FORALL and ISALL** Both of these are equivalent to their lower-case SIMPLE forms, but they are written differently.
**R, P, PP, R** is used as a predicate symbol, and its arguments' values are requested from the keyboard when the relation is executed. P and PP are predicate symbols which always return a true answer, and as a by-product print the values of their arguments. P leaves the cursor at the end of the output, and PP moves it to the next line after printing.
/* This predicate symbol causes its arguments to be disregarded, and hence act as comments.

# Chapter Seven
# AI Applications

This book can be used to lead you onto other PROLOG dialects on larger machines. In the future, the PROLOG languages will figure more and more in industry and the home, as this language is to be used within the latest 'intelligent' fifth generation machines. (The term PROLOG will often be used below, rather than micro-PROLOG, to imply that the material is not restricted to a particular dialect of PROLOG.)

There are already several systems using PROLOG in industrial applications, and this mainly stems from its use in expert systems. It is probable that the trend in the future will be for software companies to produce expert systems 'shells' which can be used to form general expert systems on any subject. An analogy to this is the spreadsheet program, which is not tied to one particular business application but can be used to construct a variety of visual structures with the computer's aid.

The main applications of PROLOG are in areas where a set of rules is to be used to make decisions. We have seen simple examples of parsing, for instance, and have touched on expert systems. We will look further at this latter area shortly. However, PROLOG is as general a computer language as any other, and in principle there is nothing which it cannot do. It is fair to say, of course, that there are tasks for which it is not easily suited, and this is true of any computer language.

### Artificial intelligence

There are many books and articles on AI, and if you are interested in pursuing this field any further the book which is considered to be a standard work is *Artificial Intelligence* by Patrick Henry Winston, published by Addison-Wesley. The book is complex and fairly deep in its approach, as well as having one of the best bibliographies and general literature references you will find. It is recommended for anyone who is serious about the subject. Another important book, which takes the reader further into the realms of micro-PROLOG and its applications, is Clarke and McCabe's *micro-PROLOG: programming in logic*, published by Prentice-Hall. This also takes some of the examples in Winston's work, and rewrites them for micro-PROLOG. Other books of interest include Mike James's *Artificial Intelligence in BASIC*, published by Newnes. This highly readable book provides some interesting examples using the most familiar of programming languages.

AI is hard to define, and it is best described by cataloguing some of its applications, some of which have already been mentioned. AI is quite widespread, and includes business applications such as expert systems and the more intelligent word processing, as well as the somewhat futuristic applications of robotic vision and computer speech recognition. It is important to realise that the concept of pattern recognition is basic to a number of AI areas. Recognition of general patterns is not restricted to computer vision; there are patterns in speech, the sense of touch, games, and many other areas which will be used in robotics and computers in the future.

One of the more interesting tasks for which computers are being used is the recognition and processing of patterns which result from taking pictures using video cameras. Applications of such processing include counting blood cells under a microscope, helping a robotic hand to locate its target, or generally recognising how many squares, circles and other geometric patterns there are in a given picture. Examination for faults in a manufacturing process is an important use too. For instance, if a machine is making a given type of biscuit, it is not difficult to pass the finished product across the field of view of a video camera, and program the computer to recognise if a biscuit has the wrong shape, and must be rejected. This is a case of stored facts being used for comparison, and has a general similarity to the PROLOG approach.

AI is also used in games playing. This is a serious subject, and has applications in any system where strategies are required. The basic examples used for developing this field often appear frivolous, but the principles learnt are basic to our conception of human intelligence, with its creativity and ability to think laterally. Games playing involves the use of such concepts as strategies and 'heuristics'. We shall look at this shortly.

As mentioned before, one of the prime tasks of AI is to enable computers to communicate freely and easily with humans. This implies the need for parsing, use of vocabulary, building up sentences from scratch to express an idea, and a certain amount of creativity. PROLOG is very well suited to this type of task. In fact, we use a PROLOG-type process ourselves while understanding speech. As we listen, or read, our brains effectively appeal to a complex set of stored rules and facts to comprehend the data. These rules are stored on our internal database by experience, and you can see this process occurring as a child learns to speak, and then later learns to read.

There are many more fields in the study of AI, but the above will give you some idea of the main components. We will now look at some of the details of two of these areas.

## Games playing

The theory of games has been studied for many years as part of mathematics. It is only comparatively recently that sophisticated, and generally available, computing power has supplied the tools for solving games problems in everyday life. A good example of this is the upsurge of chess playing computers which can be bought for a few pounds, and are capable of beating many levels of player. The computing power which goes into this type of games playing is enormous, but we often take it for granted. However, it demonstrates the fact that once a given problem is solved (even partially), it never needs to be solved again; it can be transferred from one machine to another by mechanical modification, and even appear on the cheapest and simplest machines.

The solving of games playing in general has great application in science and business. For instance, such diverse fields as solving problems in genetics, or finding the best schedule for a complex production process, provide examples which can be attacked by playing a type of game. There are also many methods of solving games problems, and indeed many classes of games to play. For instance, in games such as patience or solitaire, the player is just trying to achieve a goal from some initial state by making single moves. He is not in competition. In games such as chess or noughts and crosses, however, each player is trying to win, and at the same time trying to make life difficult for his opponent. In such cases, each move is designed, ideally, to maximise the chances of success whilst minimising the opponent's chances. This can be solved using methods known as 'minimax' principles. Many games can be represented by 'trees', where each branch of the tree denotes a possible move, and takes the game from one state to another.

Illustrating problems in games theory can quickly become highly mathematical, leading into areas such as predicate calculus, and general mathematical logic. We will steer clear of the theory, and illustrate some of the basic ideas by looking at a simple strategy based on 'heuristics'.

A heuristic is a rule for playing a game which helps a player to win. There will, in general, be many such rules, and in a game such as chess these rules are rather difficult to specify. In a simple game, however, the heuristics can be written down as rules on a database, hence the application of PROLOG.

Before continuing, it is important to compare this method with another important games playing method – that of algorithms. An algorithm is a recipe, or sequence of events, which, if followed, leads the player to a winning state unless thwarted by an opponent. BASIC is well adapted to following algorithms, and indeed the programs you write in BASIC are examples of algorithms. The PROLOG approach, as you should know by now, is not to produce an algorithm, but rather a set of facts and rules which contribute to solving a problem by querying the database where these are held. It should also be pointed out that BASIC can be used in this manner, but it is not a natural stance for the language.

Unfortunately, there are few generally familiar simple games to illustrate this. The classic game example used in many books is that of noughts and crosses, but we will take a less common example of a game and illustrate the basic principles at the same time.

We will look here at the game of generating magic squares. These are square tables of numbers where horizontal lines, vertical lines and diagonals in the square add up to some given number. For instance, the following is a rather trivial magic square:

| | | |
|---|---|---|
| 0 | 0 | 0 |
| 0 | 0 | 0 |
| 0 | 0 | 0 |

Every line in the square adds up to zero. In fact, you can quickly see that all constant value squares are 'magic'. For instance:

| | | | |
|---|---|---|---|
| 6 | 6 | 6 | 6 |
| 6 | 6 | 6 | 6 |
| 6 | 6 | 6 | 6 |
| 6 | 6 | 6 | 6 |

All lines here add up to 24.

The trick is to find magic squares where the digits are not all the same, if possible. These numbers can be positive or negative, but we will restrict ourselves to integers here.

How do we go about finding a square with a given 'value' – i.e. with all lines adding up to that number? We will attack the problem by heuristic reasoning. This involves discovering some rules which govern each move in the process. For instance, how to start would be a useful rule!

The problem is that having decided on the size of the square and the value, there is an infinite number of possible numbers which we could try in each position. In addition, you will find that if there is one solution, there is generally an infinite number of *possible* correct solutions to the problem. The general solution to the problem can be written down as a mathematical formula, and solved in that manner. However, we are illustrating games theory here, and we will take a heuristic approach which does not involve solving chains of simultaneous equations.

We could start the game by drawing a square of the right size, and then trying some numbers. The current values of the lines are calculated, and the next move is to adjust the values to bring us nearer to the result. Remember that simply because we can find a heuristic for the game does not guarantee a solution. However, a good heuristic will find a solution if it exists, though this might take a long time!

Let us look at a 3 by 3 square which has value 10. It is not possible for all the numbers in the square to be equal, because 10 is not divisible by 3 – check that you agree with this by trying it out before carrying on. To start the game, we will choose three different numbers for the top line of the square which add up to 10. In other words, we need a generating function to produce three different numbers to pass on to the rest of the play. For instance, we might choose:

| | | |
|---|---|---|
| 2 | 3 | 5 |
| . | . | . |
| . | . | . |

to start the game. If you look at this square, you should be able to see that if the middle number is chosen next, all the other numbers must come from it if there is a complete solution. For instance, if you choose 7 as the middle number to give:

| | | |
|---|---|---|
| 2 | 3 | 5 |
| . | 7 | . |
| . | . | . |

then the bottom middle number must be 0, and the two other numbers on the bottom row are fixed and calculated to ensure that the diagonals add up to 10. This finally forces the last two numbers to ensure that the left and right columns add up to 10. Unfortunately, this does not give a solution as the second two horizontal rows do not add up to 10. The numbers generated in the order suggested above will be:

| | | |
|---|---|---|
| 2 | 3 | 5 |
| 10 | 7 | 4 |
| −2 | 0 | 1 |

In fact the middle row adds up to 21 and the bottom row to −1. This means that the move was wrong, and a different number should be chosen for the central number in the square. The question is: how should we choose our next move, and then how to judge it correctly? It is easy to judge a move as right or wrong simply by filling in the numbers as shown. However, to develop a strategy, we need to find some way of choosing better and better moves – we need some way of determining the quality of a move, and refining its quality from one move to the next.

This is a general problem in games theory, and each game has its own answer to the problem. In this case, for instance, we could view the average of the values of the two incorrect rows, compared with 10, as an indicator of the nearness of the current move to the correct answer. Here this average is 10, but the answer is way out. A better indicator might be the sum of the differences between 10 and the incorrect row values. These differences are both 11 in this case, disregarding signs, and thus 22 is the value of this indicator. We should try to reduce the indicator to zero when we should have an answer to the problem. When you have the hang of this procedure, you can try choosing other numeric criteria to see if they are more efficient.

We now try another number, one more than the last one for instance, for the central position of the square, and see if this gives a complete magic square. If not, the indicator is computed and checked to see if it is better than the last one. If not, the latest guess is in the wrong direction, and it would be better to try guessing a number one less than the last guess and see if that improves matters. By this means a logical sequence of events can be used to step to the answer.

A typical sequence in this case might be to start by choosing 2 as the middle element of the square. If you perform the computation, the indicator is 8. If you try 1 as the middle element, the indicator shoots up to 14 showing that this guess is further from the correct answer. Now try 3 and 4 and the indicators will be 2 and 4 respectively. This implies that the correct middle element is somewhere between 3 and 4, but nearer to 3.

This means that there is no integer which fits, and thus a magic square with value 10 is impossible with the given top row. In fact, it can be proven by algebra that 10 is not a possible number for the value of a 3 by 3 magic square containing integers.

If a square value had been given for which there was a possible answer, then the heuristic above would have found it. As it happens, there is a simple answer to any 3 by 3 magic square. The value of the square must be divisible by 3, and the middle element is always one third of the square's value. Any one of the rows or columns can then be chosen arbitrarily, and the rest of the magic square comes from it. This is why the value 10 required a middle element near to 3 and less than 4; the value it wanted was 3.33333...

This gives a good example of the fact that though a good heuristic was chosen, its existence did not necessarily imply a solution. If it is a good heuristic, it will eventually find an existent solution.

The general solution given here for a 3 by 3 square could have been used as the basis for an algorithmic solution to the problem. A program using it is as follows:

1. If the square is 3 by 3 and value V, then end the program and print "NO SOLUTION" if V is not divisible by 3.
2. The centre element of the square is V/3.
3. The top row of the square is any three integers adding up to V.
4. The bottom row and the left and right members of the middle row are found by simple addition and subtraction.

The first rule is used to end the program if there is no solution. The next rules are never entered if this is the case. If the second rule is used the centre element of the square is calculated directly. The third rule gives a method of generating a possible top row of the square. Rule number 4 condenses the rest of the process into a single statement which says that the other members are now all found. You should try an example following these rules on a piece of paper to see their effect.

The 3 by 3 case is solved by either of the above two approaches. The case of higher magic squares is more difficult, and the general heuristic based on choosing numbers which, in some sense, move you nearer to the final answer will be useful in exploring them. The problem with the algorithmic approach is that a large amount of involved calculation or theoretical work must first be performed to find the algorithm. The heuristic approach uses trial and error and can start immediately. This is a very human approach.

micro-PROLOG can be used to solve the problem in either way. If the algorithmic method is used, then the 'is-told' relation can be used to input the square's value, and the numbers on the top row. The three rows could be considered to be three lists, from top to bottom. The first rule would be something like:

> If square value not divisible by 3 then print message: "square not possible", and end.

If the square's value is V, the second rule might be:

> The second list is (X V/3 Y)

which says that the middle element of the middle row is one third of the square's value.

The rest of the rules simply calculate the remaining elements in the second and third row. As an exercise, you should now write a program in micro-PROLOG to input a value and a top row, and then print out a magic square. As a clue, each rule you write down should calculate X, Y and Z for one of the lists, and then print it. There is no intermediate storage of values from rule to rule in micro-PROLOG, and thus the values calculated must be used immediately for printing out the answer.

The heuristic method of solving the problem will generally require a recursion to cause the program to loop towards the answer. This is also left as an exercise.

The general idea of giving a numeric value to a move is central to much of games theory. The situation becomes more complex in cases where there are two or more players opposing each other. For instance, in the perennial example of noughts and crosses, one tries to maximise one's own chances, while at the same time minimising the opponent's. To do this, it is essential to be able to give a numeric 'value' to each possible move. The best move can then be chosen and acted upon. Theoretically one's opponent should be following the same principle, of course, and the game should thus be a draw. The only way to win is to rely on a mistake by your opponent.

A numeric value may be attached to a move in noughts and crosses by calculating, for each move, how many subsequent ways there are for you and your opponent to make lines of Xs and Os respectively. The aim is to look at each possible move at any time, and choose one which maximises your number and minimises your opponent's. This is a simple example of the 'minimax' principle.

Greater complexities and chances of winning can be added by looking more than one move ahead – of course, this also requires greater memory to store the data produced, as with the recursion procedure described earlier. A game such as chess becomes impossible to compute for more than a very few moves ahead. Even in a simple game such as noughts and crosses, you find that more than two moves ahead is surprisingly difficult.

The use of the above principles brings us nearer to an understanding of intelligence. The human brain, while playing chess, is able to discard stupid lines of future moves quickly and instinctively, as if using generalised rules and facts from previous experience. The best chess programs do exactly this. Each line of future moves is examined using some general rule. If a given line appears to be heading for a dead end, it is discarded. This optimisation is intelligent, instead of just mechanical.

Games theory is a fascinating and challenging area of study which teaches us much about the way in which our brains work. By this means we hope to produce machines which are at least as clever as humans, and perhaps surpass them.

## Expert systems

The study of expert systems is often called 'knowledge engineering'. Its study is fairly well advanced, and there are many systems in existence which are useful to humans by supplying raw expert data. Such systems are not yet able to supplant human operators completely, however.

The idea is very PROLOG-like. A database is used to provide knowledge (facts) for a system which relates answers to questions to the appropriate part of the database in order to supply knowledge, and lead the user through to further pieces of information. This is a role which an expert in a given subject would normally perform. For instance, a dietary expert would ask questions and provide expertise to fit the given subject's requirements. By this process, the specific information which is required is accessed, without the person having to learn the whole subject. A similar process occurs when we use a manual to help in repairing a mechanical object. The designer of a car engine, for instance, uses thousands of pieces of data from a variety of areas of experience. To mend a car engine, however, the mechanically minded person simply follows the instructions in the book. He is accessing just the data he requires at the time, and is not interested in all of the background to the engine's design.

It is this concept of passing knowledge which is at the basis of an expert system. However, we have all observed how much more efficient that process is if some of the background is explained, instead of just gaining a few mechanical instructions on diet, or engine repairs. It is well known that the more background you have, the more useful the knowledge is. This cannot be taken to its conclusion, because we do not have enough time to become experts in all the areas of human knowledge which we need in our daily lives. A good expert system, however, is designed to allow the human operator to command it to explain the reasoning behind a given move. This is simply a question of printing out the steps it has just taken to arrive at a statement or question.

Another important aspect of an expert system is the recognition of the 'fuzzy' or inexact nature of human dealings. It is important for an expert system to be able to deal in ideas which are 'near' to each other in some sense – this is another very human attribute, and a very powerful one. It allows decisions to be based on nearness of fit which, though wrong on occasion, will be right a statistically high number of times. It should be clear to everyone that even if a book were to be completely misspelt throughout, most of its sense would actually be clear, though not all. Computer languages are, however, exact about such details as spelling, and the 'fuzzing out' of this type of exactness is important in knowledge engineering.

An important part of knowledge engineering is the acquisition stage. Experts are not necessarily the best people to design the knowledge bases of their expertise. It takes a general knowledge engineer to acquire the expert's knowledge, and an intelligent computer program to integrate it all together. One of the main uses of an expert system is to 'trap' the knowledge in a human expert, and save it from having to be rediscovered by others, perhaps when the given expert has moved away. Naturally, no-one likes to be 'mechanised', and there are some interesting social aspects to the use and building of knowledge-based systems.

Essentially, an expert system is simply an intelligent database of facts. The key is in linking the data items together. A good expert system will allow interaction with the computer in a natural language, and require no knowledge of computing. This is analogous to the need for a written engine manual in English where the book user does not need to understand printing ink chemistry, the art of typesetting, or paper technology. A good expert system will lead the user into its depths without any technical knowledge.

The basis of such a system is a set of rules on a database, some of which the user is trying to access by a question and answer session. Of course, it is too much to ask that a typical expert system should be able to accept any question; this would require a solution to the problem of intelligent communication. Instead, the expert system will generally use a simple allowable subset of a natural language, such as English, for all of its interactions with the human. In fact, it is rarely necessary to use more than a small fraction of the different vocabulary words and grammatical constructions which abound in natural language to express an idea or piece of data. Natural languages are grossly redundant. This means that a highly efficient, and fully understandable, part of a familiar language can be used with success. PROLOG is naturally orientated towards knowledge engineering. It allows facts and rules to be stored, and queries to be answered in an intelligent fashion.

To make up a simple expert system you should start off by storing facts and rules about a given subject. The next step is to consider how to access this knowledge by question and answer. This largely depends upon the way in which the rules are stored. For instance, if the subject concerned car engines, and all the rules were stored in such a way as to show how to recognise given faults, it would be unwise to start to query the database on how to repair the faults. Such queries would be answered by another database, presumably. It is important to use the data correctly, unless one has such an all-embracing system that anything can be asked about car engines.

To build up a knowledge base on engine maintenance, we could start with facts such as:

pistons move up and down
rings are placed around pistons
rings hold in the explosive gases in the chambers
petrol explodes to push the piston down
etc.

If the system were to tell the user that in its opinion the rings had gone, the user could ask where he could find these rings, so that he could repair them. The system would then consult its database, see the second rule above, and thus explain where to find the rings. This can go on more deeply into the system until the user understands enough to pick up a spanner and expose the rings for himself.

Examples of rules which help the system in diagnosis would be:

if blue smoke from exhaust then could be broken rings
if loses oil and blue smoke then broken rings or pistons
if knocking under load then could be worn big ends
if oil pressure low then could be worn big ends
if oil pressure low then could be worn main bearings

These rules, along with the facts, are the basic data of the knowledge base. Using this data in questions or answers should lead the system to a diagnosis, and give an explanation of the problem. Another set of data would be used to lead the user through the dismantling of the engine, and its subsequent repair. This type of intelligent manual could be of immense benefit to repair shops employing young inexperienced people. It allows the experience from the older hands to be shared with anyone, without occupying their time.

It is fair to say that no system is perfect, and it is not suggested that this system can yet replace the human expert. However, the saving in time and energy can enable a very few experienced people to handle a large number of others all at the same time. The savings which can accrue are enormous.

You can see how important the art of communication is to an expert system. This is the reason for assuming a set language for the communication. The ultimate goal is to produce expert systems which can parse and construct general natural language questions and answers during a session.

You should be able to construct the elements of a simple expert system in PROLOG, and you should choose a subject you know something about. Begin by writing down a few straightforward truths about your subject as facts. Do not use too many different verbs, and write the sentences in a simple form. To do this, you will have to break complex ideas into smaller more manageable units.

Then consider some rules which link ideas together. Use purely 'if... then ...' structures, perhaps with 'and' and 'or' connectives, as in micro-PROLOG. This will give you a basis of rules. Now construct some simple queries to show that the data 'works'.

The next step is to make the jump into a true expert system by constructing routines which ask the user questions, demanding that the answers conform to a simple pattern of sentences, and using a minimum number of verbs and nouns. Given these answers, your program should access the stored rules and facts to lead onto further questions. The natural backtracking nature of micro-PROLOG will help to ensure that few stones are left unturned by this process.

The next step is to be able to command the system to repeat its reasoning for coming to a given conclusion. This is not simple; it involves tracing back through a complex sequence of operations and printing out the intermediate stages.

Some expert systems allow a statistical element to be included in the rules and facts. For instance, an engine repair rule might be stated as:

```
if blue smoke then broken rings (prob. 0.8)
                   broken pistons (prob. 0.4)
                   oil on exhaust manifold (prob. 0.1)
```

All the information given here can be accessed, and used by the querying routine to build up a most probable cause, after some further questions have been asked.

## Conclusion

Slowly but surely computers, or rather their programs, are becoming more and obviously intelligent. In order to appreciate this intelligence fully, it becomes increasingly important to be able to communicate with computers naturally. This is one of the reasons for the central role of list processing in AI. However, some branches do not need this yet. Computer vision and general pattern recognition are, arguably, two of them. Similarly, the intelligent control of robotic machinery is another, though it is most people's conception of a robot that it should be able to communicate directly with humans. Anything less is not considered to be fully intelligent.

In any case AI, as with any other field of human endeavour, will not receive the boost it needs until the politicians and other non-technical decision makers are captured, in some way, by the field. Imagine how impressive will be the first robot which, however awkwardly, saunters up to the Prime Minister and begins a meaningful dialogue on the subject of the problems of the Third World or the vagaries of Government spending on manufacturing industry!

# Index